polenta

100 Innovative Recipes
From Appetizers to Desserts

p o l e n t a

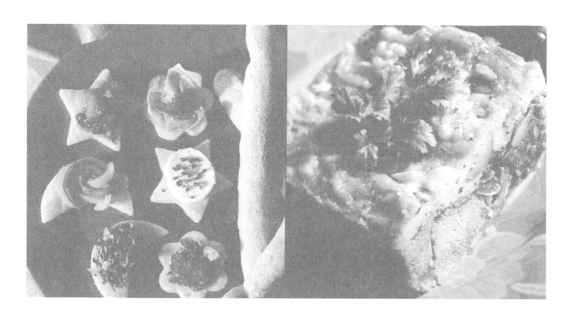

Michele Anna Jordan

BROADWAY BOOKS   NEW YORK

BROADWAY

FIRST EDITION

Designed by Bonni Leon-Berman

Library of Congress Cataloging-in-Publication Data

Jordan, Michele Anna.
   Polenta : 100 innovative recipes, from appetizers to desserts /
Michele Anna Jordan. — 1st ed.
     p. cm.
   Includes bibliographical references.
   ISBN 0-553-06732-X (hardcover)
   1. Polenta. I. Title.
TX809.M2J67   1997
641.6'315—dc20   96-31712
                            CIP

97 98 99 00 10 9 8 7 6 5 4 3 2 1

"Just finish it," his e-mails encouraged. "Quit accepting invitations and finish *Polenta*," he urged in the fall of '95, not once but frequently, speaking straight to the heart of my procrastination. Thanks, John, for prodding me to stick to it, and for all of your sage advice and concern, past, present, and future.

and in memory of Mathilda,

1981–1996,

a sweet feline, indeed

c o n t e n t s

POLENTA is one of those ageless culinary lords, like bread. It has sprung from the hunger of mankind, and without apparent effort has always carried with it a feeling of strength and dignity and well-being.

It costs little to prepare, if there is little to spend, or it can be extravagantly, opulently odorous with wines and such. It can be made doggedly, with one ear cocked for the old wolf's sniffing under the door, or it can be turned out as a well-nourished gesture to other simpler days. But no matter what conceits it may be decked with, its fundamental simplicity survives, to comfort our souls as well as our bellies, the way a good solid fugue does, or a warm morning in spring.

—M.F.K. Fisher, *How to Cook a Wolf*, 1942

a c k n o w l e d g m e n t s

In a sense, Polenta was an easy book to write: my crew of tasters has never before been so eager to sample recipes. Thanks to everyone for eating and overeating and then eating even more polenta: Mary and Guy Duryee, Jerry and Patty Hertz, John Gordon (whose translations helped, too), Miriam Silver, Keith and Evelyn Anderson, and all of the other brave palates. Easy?" I can hear my assistant Betty Ellsworth saying as she laughs. Heaps of thanks to Betty for keeping me sane, for her fearless organization skills (not to mention talent for interpreting my recipes), and most importantly, for the warmth and friendship that sustains me. Lesa Tanner, too, adds invaluable assistance. *Thanks, again.* And a special acknowledgment and huge hug goes out to Evelyn Anderson, producer of my radio show *Mouthful,* who works harder than anyone putting together the show (and occasionally, me). And thanks to Robin Pressman, too, program director at KRCB-FM, for encouraging and supporting *Mouthful.* And to Ginny Stanford, there is not a big enough thank you to cover it all: I leave it to your understanding to know just what I want to say. Thanks a million to my agent Doe Coover and to Harriet Bell, my editor at Broadway Books. I feel truly blessed to work with such great people. I also want to extend my gratitude to Elizabeth Carduff of Addison-Wesley Publishing Co., whose enthusiasm for polenta launched this project years ago. Elizabeth also introduced me to the work of photographer Tom Eckerle, who produced the striking photographs here. Several groups and individuals provided products during the recipe-testing and photography phases of the project, and I thank them here: Manicaretti Imports, the California Milk Advisory Board, Gray's Gristmill, and The Polenta Company. And huge thanks to the Italian Trade Commission for arranging my polenta adventures in Italy. *Mille grazie* to the Traverso family, who came to Sonoma County from Genoa in the 1920s and established Traverso's Market in 1932. At a time when shopping has become increasingly impersonal—generic foods housed in cavernous warehouses, clerks who don't even look at you, let alone know your name or remember your favorite cheese—markets like Traverso's are more important than ever. A highlight of my day comes whenever I walk through the door and am greeted by Rico or Louie, whose father founded the store, or by George or Bill, their sons who now manage the family operation. Through the Traversos, I have learned much of what I know. The human element, the sense of inclusion and family, the warmth that permeates the store, have been as crucial to me as the mozzarella and olive oil, the polenta and prosciutto, the cannellini beans and pancetta, that have become my daily fare. I would be lost without the market, but I would be sad indeed without the warmth and kindness the Traversos and their staff have shown me all these years. *Finally*, to my daughters Gina and Nicolle, and my dear friends, James Carroll and John Boland: *I couldn't do any of this without you.* I hope you know that.

Introduction

*W*hy a book on polenta, I've asked myself more times than I really care to admit. If there is a drop of Italian blood in these veins, there are no known ancestors to claim it. I did not eat cornmeal mush as a child, and do not, in fact, recall a single fragrant square of cornbread. I was a young adult before I encountered polenta for the first time. *O*ne day in the mid-1970s, I bought a sack of polenta from my local Italian market, cooked some according to directions in whatever Italian cookbook was on the shelf, and poured it into a gelatin mold. When it was ready to hold its shape, I inverted it onto a pretty plate and dusted the top with freshly grated cheese. I was not a professional cook at that time, merely an enthusiastic one who forged ahead wherever my inclinations took me, oblivious of the world's culinary traditions, trends, and fashions. *P*olenta was remarkably easy to make from the start, adapted well to a sauce, and produced consistently wonderful results. I have not gone long without polenta since that first time, and I have even become somewhat of a polenta proselytizer. *Polenta* is a product of this enthusiasm, of my conviction that polenta is not only a breeze to prepare, but that adding it to your repertoire will expand your cooking horizons deliciously. For all its regional names and contemporary romance, polenta is simply cornmeal stirred and simmered in a liquid. *I*n all likelihood, I encountered cornmeal mush in my youth. I can't imagine that I wouldn't have, but I had an aversion to many sweets, a prejudice I still carry, and therein lies its absence from my early years. All efforts to get me to eat oatmeal, wheat hearts, or any of the sweet morning comfort foods that sustain whole populations failed utterly. Then, as now, if I wanted anything at all, I wanted it salty; nothing pleased me so much as simple toasted bread with butter. Whatever odd chemistry eclipsed my innate human sweet tooth, I cannot tell you, but I do suspect that it is what kept me from cornmeal. As a breakfast tradition in America, cornmeal is served with milk and sugar, honey, or jam. Today, I delight in a bowl of steaming polenta on a cold morning, topped not with syrup or sugar but with toasted walnuts, butter, and Gorgonzola cheese. Polenta is, more than anything, an exploration of cornmeal's endless savory possibilities. My closest childhood connection to the ancient corn culture was through popcorn. If my mother had a culinary legacy, she never shared it, and I was on my own in the kitchen at a very young age, first crawling up onto the counter to stand precariously on the edge of the sink and peer into the top cupboards nearly beyond my reach to search for treasures. A hidden stash of cornmeal was not among the spoils. By my eighth birthday, a neighbor had given me a child's cookbook and, along with it, tacit approval for my eager explorations. It wasn't long before I had created a few corn rituals, though I didn't think of them as such. I simply enjoyed making popcorn sculptures. In the solitude of the kitchen I would fashion the corn into simple commemorative figures. After popping a batch, I stirred food coloring into a bubbling cauldron of corn syrup and sugar, barely able to reach the spoon down into the pot. Next, I would drop in the popcorn, give it an awkward stir, and dump it onto a piece of wax paper spread on the table. I would rub my hands liberally with butter and sculpt the hot, sweet mass into Halloween pumpkins, Christmas trees, snowmen, and huge abstract Easter eggs. One Valentine's Day, a child in love, I made a large red popcorn heart. Of course, I knew nothing then of the long parade of corn drawings, sculptures, statues, castles, and other simple and sophisticated representations of corn reaching all the way back to the beginnings of human civilization, nor was there any grand meaning or transcendental implication in what I did. I simply loved what I was doing. As a child bride, a teenage mother, I continued my corn-sculpting rituals. I awoke one chilly December morning at 5 A.M. with the first pangs of impending birth. In twenty-four hours, my first daughter would be born. But first there were matters to tend to. By the time the anemic winter sun had risen, freshly popped corn, as pristine as snow, sat on the table. I stirred the corn syrup, sugar, and food coloring, struggling with the pot because of the size of my belly, a plump kernel indeed, ready to spill forth. And so there I sat at a little kitchen table, timing my contractions while I shaped Christmas popcorn for my young husband, thousands of miles away. Among my creations were a popcorn snowman, a Christmas tree, and several popcorn snowballs, along with some carefully cut and painted Christmas cookies. I packaged things up and got them to the post office before I even contemplated going to the hospital. A personal birth rite, you could say, a small, inarticulate ritual; silent, ignorant of the grand corn culture whose celebrations I intuitively mimicked, however modestly. In my pursuit of the polenta story, I was led quickly, inevitably, to corn and its tale. Polenta is but a chapter in the grand corn opus, which in turn is a human story, an intimate saga of our own history. Wherever you look, there it is again, corn, inextricably linked with humankind, ancient and modern, providing us with everything from sweet corn snapped from its stalk and devoured immediately to animal feed, fabric, fiber, fuel, and dozens of other nonculinary but essential necessities. The same is true with recipes. They just keep coming—as found objects and sudden inspirations. Flavors pass through time and culture, wave upon wave of fashionable aromas and trendy flavors to enchant us. The very language of the day inspires those of us who cook not from recipes but from our own internal cookbook. So often, I hear a simple mention of an ingredient or cooking technique, and suddenly I am daydreaming.

The new recipe is my own in one sense, but from a broader view it belongs as much to the culture as it does to me. Who first thought of mango salsa, garlic mashed potatoes, lavender ice cream, pizza crust made with polenta? Does it really matter, could we even discover an original source? However, whenever I am aware of my inspiration, I have credited the culture, the chef, the writer, or the book. Nothing—except brand names and marketing tactics—is new, it is simply reborn as each generation explores its inheritances and makes its own discoveries, reinventing ancient flavor combinations in the process. Today, we think that we've invented, say, flavored vinegars and mustards, yet they were tremendously popular in both Europe and the United States as late as the 1940s, when there were more than a dozen flavors of vinegar produced in the United States alone. A hundred years ago in France, the selection of flavored mustards—rose petal and vanilla among them—was even more diverse than what we find on market shelves today. And now corn is on the rise again. Corn, including polenta, belongs to each of us, as indeed it always has in some form or another. Each of us has our personal corn heritage because corn and humankind are simply inseparable. I say, catch the wave this time around, if you have not already done so. You'll make polenta your own in no time.

all about polenta

Il paiolo, heavy with glittering yellow cornmeal, is hauled from the fireplace to the *madia,* a beechwood cupboard where flour and bread are stored. A cloud of vapor envelops both the paiolo and the cook, who carefully tips the pounded copper cauldron and pours the fragrant, steaming mass on the top of the wooden cupboard. Steam rises, surrounding the golden halo of soft cooked corn: Italy's harvest moon rising out of a mist of fog, says Alessandro Manzoni, Italy's great nineteenth-century novelist. *Ahh, polenta.* When the hearth was the center of the home, this was a scene you could find throughout northern Italy. Stories abound of the unlined copper kettle with its curved bottom and long handle, the hours of conversation around the hearth, while the family warmed itself and Mamma or Nonna tirelessly stirred the cornmeal until it pulled away cleanly from the sides of the kettle, tender, soft, and fragrant. More than the visual cue—which can be deceptive; perhaps the polenta is only parched, in need of a splash of water—it was Mamma's subtle intuitive sense of the corn itself that would tell her it was time for the big round golden circle surrounded by foggy vapor to stir the palates of the family just as it stirred the imaginations of a myriad of poets, writers, and artists. Not only are there dozens of hearty recipes passed on from these cozy hearths, there are scores of literary, musical, and artistic references—poems and stories, paintings, novels, and songs—that evoke polenta's inexhaustible power to comfort and please and nourish. Call it whatever you like—polenta, mush, cornmeal, *mamaliga, las pous*—polenta is the ultimate comfort food. Polenta can be a cook's best friend—or certainly one of them. It can be served right from the stove with butter and cheese or poured onto a board and cut with a wire, as was the custom so long ago. It can set up in a mold—

plain or fancy—later to be sliced and fried, broiled, or grilled, and crowned with a savory sauce. A pot of hot bubbling polenta is the culinary equivalent of an artist's canvas, waiting for a cook to contribute his or her magic. In the last decade, polenta has become astonishingly popular in America, though it always has been around in one form or another. But now it transcends its humble origins as mush, suppawn, or hasty pudding. It is featured in everything from pizza crust to shortcake, paired with such luxurious ingredients as caviar and lobster. It is on the menus of the best restaurants, new cookbooks pay homage to it, recipes for it appear regularly in virtually every food publication in the country. At the Clinton White House, at a state dinner honoring Oscar Scalfaro, president of Italy, polenta was seasoned with fresh basil and served with portobello mushrooms. In the spring of 1996, an Internet search revealed more than two thousand references to polenta. This is not to say that polenta has become a pantry staple in our home kitchens. For the most part, home cooks still find it intimidating. Just consider the plastic tubes and blocks of prepared polenta available in supermarkets and the boxes of instant polenta that line the shelves. The mystique of polenta, the image of that paiolo and the constant stirring, stirring, stirring it demanded, makes a bowl of fragrant, steamy polenta seem an illusive, luxurious pleasure. How sad and how untrue. With the consistent heat provided by modern cookstoves and with modern cooking equipment, it is extremely easy to make a bowl of polenta a weekly or even a daily reality, should you be so inclined. If you insist on the traditional technique, there is even a motorized paiolo to do the stirring for you. This image of constant stirring is largely a romantic one. The technique works, certainly, and there are times when it is appropriate, such as when preparing an enormous pot of polenta for several dozen guests. Then, nearly constant stirring is necessary to cook the polenta evenly, to move the cornmeal from the bottom to the top of the pot, from the sides of the pot to the middle, continually circulating the meal to ensure that the bottom does not burn while the top languishes undone. But how often do you cook polenta for a hundred, or even twenty, people? Besides, it is the tradition at such gatherings for each of the revelers to take a turn at the stick. Polenta for two, polenta for four, polenta for six: it is very simple indeed. Yet the baton, the paddle, the thick wooden spoon should not be banished to the museum of culinary relics. The slow stirring of polenta has another important function: it relieves stress and lightens depression. There are times when we all long to retreat from the world, from its demands and pace, however briefly. You simply can't beat the soothing tonic of stirring a fragrant pot of bubbling cornmeal. Suddenly, the world is reduced to a small sphere of warmth, aroma, and hypnotic motion; cares drift away on a fragrant cloud of steam and you find yourself relaxing in spite of your troubles. And unlike certain other escapes—television, a martini or two, Prozac—you are returned to the world with a tangible, albeit humble, accomplishment: a pot of perfectly cooked polenta. This is the time to make two, three, four times the amount you need for one meal: pour what you don't eat immediately into tart shells, fancy molds, and baking sheets for use over the next several days. Wrapped tightly in plastic, your polenta will take you through the week. However you get your polenta to the table, it links you with traditions that stretch back not mere decades or centuries but millennia, before a single stalk of corn flowered in European soil.

Polenta Before Corn

Before corn came to Europe, there was polenta and before polenta, there were *puls* and *pulmentum*, Roman names for a porridge, similar to polenta, made with millet, chest-

In 1793, New England revolutionary Joel Barlow, Betty Fussell tells us in *The Story of Corn* (Knopf, 1992), was traveling in the Savoie in eastern France when he came upon a bowl of *polente au bâton* and "was straightway seized by homesickness and the muse." Given to writing epics like *The Vision of Columbus*, he now tore off several hundred mock-epic lines on the subject of mush. "The soft nations round the warm Levan' call it *Polenta*," Barlow said approvingly, "the French, of course, *Polente*." But his fellow Americans embarrassed him by the vulgarity of their tongue: "Ev'n in thy native regions, how I blush / To hear the Pennsylvanians call thee Mush!"

Not all cultures welcome polenta, nor relish their reliance upon it. The Irish version, for example, known as *stirrabout*, was eaten to ward off starvation and seen as a humble food. To acknowledge eating it was once considered a humiliating admission of poverty, a bias that lingers.

Africa Frou Frou, Kenkey, Posho (Swahili), Putu (Bantu)

Barbados Coo Coo

Boston Indian Pudding, Hasty Pudding

Classical Pulse, Pulmentum, Poltos

France
   Béarn Broye
   Gascony Armottes
   Landes Cruchade
   Languedoc Rimotes; Milhas
   Southwest Millas
   Périgord Las Pous
   Savoie Polente

Georgia Gomi

Holland Sapahn

Hungary and Rumania Kalderash, Mamaliga

Ireland Stirrabout

Italy Polenta, Polentina

New England Suppawn

Pennsylvania Mush

Transylvania Puliszka

West Indies Konkies

Sources: *The Story of Corn* (Knopf, 1992); *The Cooking of South-West France* (Dial, 1983); *The Food of Italy* (Vintage, 1977); *Of Soda Bread and Guinness* (Bobbs-Merrill, 1973)

nut flour, chick-pea flour, roasted barley, and other grains. Preparation was virtually identical to polenta, and the mixture of ground grain and water was frequently flavored and fortified with milk, cheese, and meats or their sauces. The Greeks, who knew it as *poltos*, made it with spelt flour, a larger and harder grain than our wheat, also called *farro*. Two centuries before the arrival of corn, buckwheat—known as *grano saraceno* in Italy—made its way to Europe, introduced by the Saracens, who brought it from central Asia. It was prepared in very much the same way as chestnut flour and barley, and as corn would be. Called both *polenta nera* and *polenta taragna*, it remains popular in certain regions of Italy today, Tuscany among them, and the grain is sometimes added to cornmeal for additional flavor, as in Bergamo. In virtually every culture the world around, you will find a similar comfort food, a porridge or pudding or gruel, served soft or allowed to harden, made of the common grain of the land.

Corn Reaches Italy and Returns to the New World as Polenta

The history of corn, the story of its origins, migration, and insinuation into every aspect of human life the globe around, is no simple tale. It is a deceptively complex subject, and as I attempted to get my arms around the New World's most remarkable contribution to humanity, corn instead got its arms around me. ". . . like Captain Ahab's monstrous whale," Betty Fussell writes in *The Story of Corn*, "[corn] possesses its pursuers until it drives them mad." Today, anyone flirting with the topic—and flirting, indeed, is what I have done (I cannot claim consummation)—owes an enormous debt as much to Ms. Fussell's passion, who by her own admission is infected with corn madness, as to her exhaustive research. When seeking a quick resolution to the inquiry "What, exactly, is corn?," it is wise to heed her warnings. "Corn breeds its own poets, lunatics and lovers.

After five years of corn madness, I can't think of anything sexier than corn. Or more dangerous." Proceed with caution, she implies. Wanton corn, a seed so eager to grow that it will sprout virtually anywhere it is dropped; clever corn, so versatile a plant that the 3 pounds a day Americans consume in some form or another make up less than 1 percent of the 100 million metric tons produced here each year; capricious corn, which makes a contribution to everything from lipstick, rubber tires, embalming fluid, and aspirin tablets to shotgun shells, dynamite, books, penicillin, aluminum, and whiskey, to name a few products that rely upon corn; a substance this malleable does not readily give up its secrets. For our exploration of polenta, we must distill the larger story, skim off a bit of froth from a beguiling, gurgling cauldron of corn and its myriad incarnations. Corn, *Zea mays,* is one of three related species of grass, all native to the Americas; one variety, popcorn, was cultivated at least as early as 3500 B.C. A pervasive corn culture, its roots sunk deep into prehistory, had firm hold in the New World long before Christopher Columbus, Hernando Cortés, and their compatriots found their way to these shores. Corn was used wisely and well long before Europeans saw their first kernel. Although there are varying accounts of how many kernels of corn made it across the Atlantic, we know that Columbus returned to Barcelona with some from his first voyage to the New World. One of the more romantic stories has him carrying a few kernels in his pocket, precious seeds that upon sprouting gave birth to the vast corn culture of Europe. More than a few seeds made the journey, but whether a handful or a cargo hold's worth, seed corn had indeed landed on European shores, where it was soon grown as animal feed. Initially viewed with suspicion, corn nonetheless traveled quickly throughout western and portions of eastern Europe. Certain cultures, most notably Spain, have never thoroughly abandoned their view of corn as animal fodder. Spain does not have a corn culture to speak of, a curious fact in light of the importance of corn in the lands Spain conquered so successfully. Where in Italy did corn make its first appearance? Because corn quickly became known as *granoturco,* it seems likely that it arrived through the port of Venice, where trading with Turkey as well as other countries was brisk.

The name has been used as evidence that corn traveled to Italy from Asia rather than the New World, though nothing supports this claim. The trail of corn, if not its name, leads reliably to Columbus and the West Indies. It wasn't long before the Italians, who embraced so many New World commodities with a hungry enthusiasm, became adept at preparing corn, dried and ground into meal, for their tables. Italian historians believe that it was Piero Gaioncelli of Bergamo, an adventurous traveler who followed in the tracks of Columbus, who first imported and cultivated corn in the province of Bergamo, initially in Gandino and then on a farm between Volpino and Lovere around 1658. "We hope he was also the first, and here history fails us," the polenta historians say, "to produce its flour and make polenta. Should this not be the case, fate would have been cruel to him, denying him that pleasure that, thanks to him, his fellow countrymen subsequently enjoyed!" Between the seventeenth and eighteenth centuries, polenta became the culinary mainstay of the mountain and peasant populations of northern Italy. By the eighteenth century, polenta was so widely used, not only as a food but as a source of inspiration for poets, writers, artists, and musicians, that the period is frequently called the Golden Age of Polenta. Yet in the south, where Spaniards brought corn to Sicily, it was used primarily as a decorative plant. To this day, southern Italians refer disparagingly to northerners as "polenta eaters." If Columbus was a grand success securing corn from the New World, he was a dismal failure when it came to importing the native wisdom that accompanied its use. In nutritional terms, corn has a few inconvenient deficiencies: it lacks tryptophan, lysine, and niacin, essential amino acids. Left to subsist solely on corn, the human body quickly deteriorates from a lack of niacin. American Indian cultures apparently sensed this; virtually all societies that relied on corn as a major part of their diet combined it with some form of alkaline, which alters the chemistry of corn, allowing tryptophan to be converted into usable niacin, an amino acid that is essential to virtually all human metabolic processes. In the winter months when little other than polenta was available, peasant populations of northern Italy grew ill with a disease called pellagra, or "rough skin." Skin rashes and sores are among the many symptoms of pellagra; others include diarrhea, dizziness, nervousness, and mental deterioration. Initially these ailments were thought to be brought on by the consumption of corn, and for a time the eating of polenta was forbidden in Italy. There were outbreaks of pellagra in numerous parts of the world, including France, Africa, and eventually the United States, where southern sharecroppers suffered in great numbers. Scientists worked for decades to discover the cause, but it was not until the twentieth century and the discovery of niacin in the late 1930s that pellagra was confirmed to be a disease of nutritional deficiency. However, pellagra did not diminish the popularity of corn, or decrease the use of its ground meal for polenta. By the early nineteenth century, American cookery books included recipes not only for hasty pudding, Indian pudding, and other variations of sweet cornmeal porridges, but also for cornmeal flavored with butter and cheese. Some of these recipes called for the cornmeal to be set up, sliced, and fried. These early American recipes for savory cornmeal referred to the dish as polenta, the Old World's gift, however ironic, to the New World.

Corn, Polenta, and Health

Corn is high in protein, from 10 to 20 percent depending on the variety; it contains a moderate amount of dietary fiber and significant amounts of carbohydrate, vitamin C, folic acid, magnesium, phosphorus, and thiamine. Yet it is deficient in the essential amino acids tryptophan and lysine. And although corn contains a considerable amount of vitamin B_3, niacin, a lack of which is responsible for pellagra, it is in a form that cannot be absorbed by humans. When corn is combined with an alkaline substance such as ash or lime, and ground into tortilla flour, the niacin is made available for human use. As Harold McGee explains in *On Food and Cooking,* "alkaline conditions release corn's bound niacin, which can then be absorbed and used by the body." Corn, like other plant foods, has a negligible amount of fat and contains no cholesterol. One cup of cooked yellow polenta contains about 120 calories and not quite 3 grams of protein. As a grain, corn has an important role in the Mediterranean diet, which has enjoyed tremendous press in recent years, as well it should. Not only is there substantial evidence of the health benefits of a diet high in plant-based foods, it is easy to maintain and thoroughly delightful to eat. Keep its basic structure in mind as you plan menus: make olive oil your primary fat; include an abundance of complex carbohydrates such as breads, grains, including polenta, beans, and pasta; serve a salad at every meal; use a wide variety of vegetables; serve meat only occasionally, but serve cheese and yogurt regularly; enjoy wine as a regular part of meals; and don't forget to exercise. Because polenta adapts so well to other ingredients, including olive oil, beans, other legumes, and vegetables, it is—or can be—an invaluable component of a healthy diet.

Commercial Polenta Production

Across the United States, from Calistoga, California, in the heart of the wine country, to Adamsville, Rhode Island, and Midland City, Alabama, small stone grist mills grind dried corn and other grains much as has been done for centuries. Some, such as Calistoga's Grist Mill, which sits inside a state park, are true antiques, without phones or other modern amenities. To purchase grains from this mill, you must go to the facility. Others have operated continuously for centuries, small commercial ventures that have passed from owner to owner but never ceased operations. These mills offer a handful of premium products far better than anything we can purchase at a supermarket, and many are available by mail order. It is among these artisan grains that you will find polenta with the truest corn flavor. The techniques of the old grist mills are similar, in that the process involves the grinding of whole grain between heavy stones. Yet exactly how this is accomplished and with what source of power varies a great deal. Bob and Diane Smith of Carpenter's Grist Mill, founded in 1701, operate with water power, which poses challenges in

MAMALIGA

To the casual observer, there are few differences between eastern European *mamaliga* and Italian polenta. Yet Moldavians insist that their version is far better, crediting the superiority of the local bright orange stone-ground cornmeal. Preparation techniques are similar, though not identical. Cornmeal for mamaliga is cooked in boiling, salted water, but after the cornmeal is incorporated into the liquid, the pot is covered and left to simmer until it has thickened, about ten minutes. Next, butter is added and the mixture is stirred for another five minutes or so. The mamaliga is then poured into a bowl and left briefly to set up. It is served inverted onto a plate, and melted butter is poured over it.

There are several variations to this basic preparation. Feta cheese is crumbled over the surface and the mamaliga is baked in a hot oven until the cheese is melted. It is then served with melted butter. It might also be sliced, fried in butter, and served with bacon. Alternately, a sandwich may be made with two slices of mamaliga, a slice of ham, and a slice of sharp cheese. The sandwich is then dipped in egg and fried. Another variation features hot mamaliga mixed with kasseri cheese and garlic butter, and then baked until the top is golden brown. Like its Italian counterpart, mamaliga also is served with hearty stews and meat sauces and with powdered sugar or jam for dessert.

the fall when leaves and twigs must be continuously removed, and in the winter, when they must break the ice before they can begin to grind their corn. Whitecap flint corn, grown on their farm, dries in a corn crib for about six months, during which time it is measured for moisture to determine when it is ready to be ground. This is Rhode Island's native corn, cultivated long before Europeans arrived and used in the state's signature johnnycakes. Not far from Carpenter's Mill is Gray's Gristmill, operated for the last fifteen years by Tim McTague, who runs it for his friend Ralph Guild, who purchased it from John Hart. Hart and his father operated Gray's, the oldest continuously run mill in the United States, for nearly a century before selling it to Guild. Tim was twenty-three when he took over, and Hart remained to pass on his techniques and knowledge to the young miller. Gray's mill is powered by an International M 1949 tractor, which replaced the old Dodge truck engine that supplied the power for years. The mill produces several products that McTague calls "swamp Yankee food, the foods from the Colonial period," including johnnycake meal, brown bread mix, rye flour, wheat flour, white cornmeal, and yellow cornmeal. As interest increased, he also began producing a very coarse-ground polenta. The polenta is remarkable both for the size of its grains, considerably larger than any other I have encountered, and for its voluptuous corn flavor. McTague uses organic yellow dent corn from Champlain Valley Milling Corporation in Westport, New York. It arrives at Gray's Gristmill cleaned, shelled, and dried. McTague feeds the large kernels between the milling stones, packages it, and mails it out immediately. Clearly proud of his craft, McTague tells of a letter he received from Julia Child praising his cornmeal, which she uses for polenta, the letter says. Cookbook author Paula Wolfert has requested custom-ground polenta from Gray's. It seems that chefs from around the country are discovering this polenta, which poses a new difficulty. Can McTague increase production while maintaining quality? He is determined to do so. Artisan-crafted polentas, like artisan olive oils, vinegars, and other products, are wonderful when you can find them and if you can afford them. But most of us must rely on mass-produced products from large companies. Increasingly, there is good-quality polenta available, made from corn that is degermed, crushed between large steel rollers, and sifted to sort the size of the grain. The largest grains are sometimes sold as polenta, sometimes as coarse-ground cornmeal. The larger the grain, the better results you will get when you prepare polenta. Try those that are available in your area—until you find a polenta that suits your palate.

How to Purchase and Store Polenta

Depending on where you live, you may or may not be able to purchase a good polenta at your local market. West of the Rockies, Golden Pheasant, a very good polenta, is widely available. Goya is a good brand available on the East Coast. Manicaretti, an import company based in South San Francisco, distributes Moretti polenta, which is available in several forms including polenta taragna, and coarse-ground white polenta, produced by Molini Riuniti of Bergamo. It is available in specialty shops and by mail-order. Mail order is often the best choice for locating outstanding polenta. There are retail catalogs that offer a good selection, as well as several small mills that will ship direct. On the other hand, because of shipping costs, this method can be pricey, which defeats the purpose of polenta as an inexpensive staple. If you must purchase by mail order, it is best to do so in larger rather than smaller quantities; buy with friends so that

Celebrations are as old as civilization, and older of course. In early history, festivities marked both natural occurrences and significant human passages. The return of the sun—that is, the lengthening of days that is perceptible shortly after the winter solstice—sparked a celebration that coincides, though not coincidentally, with the Christian Feast of the Epiphany on January 6, and can be interpreted in part as an acknowledgment of the natural event. Birth, marriage, and death, springtime, harvest, the onset of winter, the waxing and the waning of the moon, all have been commemorated throughout time with special ceremonies, dances, foods, and drink. To discover the ancient corn festivals, one must look to the native civilizations of the Americas, to the Incas and Aztecs and Mayans as well as to more recent cultures and tribes whose elaborate rituals are recorded in detail in *The Story of Corn*.

Areas of Provence incorporate polenta into harvest festivals, but no place else celebrates the sustaining power of polenta with such flair as Italy. Italian festivals commemorate both religious and secular events, sometimes acknowledging the ways polenta has played a crucial historical role, sometimes simply including it as one of the foods of the region. On March 6 in the Piedmont town of Monastero Bormida, an enormous *polentonissimo* celebrates the generosity of Marchese Rovere, who nearly two hundred years ago saved the lives of starving coppersmiths trapped by a snowstorm by feeding them polenta in a sauce of sausage and onions. In late April another Piedmont festival honors the generosity of the ruling de Carretto family who in 1650 responded to the plight of hungry, tired coppersmiths by commissioning them to make a huge copper polenta pot. On the last Tuesday of Carnival, a particularly dramatic festival takes place in Tossignano in Emilia-Romagna. Yet another celebration of polenta rescuing a people from the brink of starvation, the *Polentata* re-creates an occasion when government used its storehouse of polenta to feed the hungry townsfolk. In Tossignano cooks prepare 440 pounds of polenta, Carol Field tells us in *Celebrating Italy*, that once cooked is layered with a sea of *ragù*, 220 pounds of sausage, 66 pounds of ground beef, 44 pounds of pancetta, and 55 pounds of grated Parmesan cheese.

Throughout the United States, numerous small towns stage polenta feeds, generally as fund-raisers for churches and other community groups, sometimes simply as a good reason to get together with friends. In Chisholm, Minnesota, Valentini's Supper Club has long held a Polenta on the Board Festival. Although the health department recently required certain changes, the original festival consisted of an enormous lake of polenta poured onto huge plywood planks set on tables. Marinara sauce was poured down the middle of the polenta and sausages were added on top. Guests pulled up chairs and tucked into the gleaming yellow mass, each person trying to be the first to eat his or her way to the center and its reward of sausages and sauce.

you can use the polenta in a timely manner. The Resources section of this book (pages 133–134) includes what I consider the best producers. Once you have secured a good polenta, it is important to keep it fresh. As pretty as a jar of golden cornmeal looks on the pantry shelf, this is not the best location for it. Polenta, especially if stone ground with its germ, will not only lose its appealing taste rapidly, it will go rancid fairly quickly. It is best to keep polenta in a sealed container in the refrigerator and use it within two months of purchase.

cooking polenta:
techniques and recipes

No other food requires such a precise ritual, such particular utensils, perfect measuring of water, salt, and flour, such scrupulous and attentive care: if today we wish to make "good" polenta, we must follow that ancient ritual, use the same equipment, the same ingredients, use the same proportions and carry out the same ancient gestures.—from The Knights of Polenta *handbook*

The source of polenta's reputation for lengthy and laborious cooking lies in its Italian roots, its history of being cooked over a wood fire in a central hearth or on a wood stove. In such circumstances, the curved bottom and long handle of the traditional polenta pot, a pounded copper cauldron called a *paiolo,* are essential. Copper conducts heat evenly, the curved bottom exposes a greater portion of the cornmeal to the heat and ensures there are no corners for the polenta to get stuck in, and the long handle keeps the cook a comfortable distance from both the fire and the sputtering cornmeal. Constant stirring with a long-handled paddle, stick, or spoon is necessary to keep the polenta from burning. Today, few of us cook over a wood fire. With easily controlled burners and heavy-bottomed pots that encourage even cooking, polenta can simmer away on its own, with occasional stirring all that is necessary. An Italian friend who remembers his grandmother's polenta suspects the constant stirring was a ruse to keep grandchildren occupied while adults tended to other matters. Be that as it may, you can easily accomplish other tasks while your polenta gurgles, plops, and spits on the stove. The larger the quantity of polenta, the more attention it requires. A huge pot to serve a couple of dozen or a couple of hundred guests needs to be stirred frequently so that it will cook evenly, but a smaller amount can be left to simmer slowly and stirred now and then while you prepare the rest of the meal. Polenta can also

Although in Italy it is illegal to kill songbirds, polenta served with grilled birds is a revered Bergamask tradition. Out of need—the region of Bergamo was until quite recently very poor—the songbirds were caught in thin nets stretched across the hilltops of Bergamo as they migrated north. After their feathers were removed—they were dressed no further—several songbirds were threaded on a single skewer. They were then grilled quickly and served over a platter of creamy polenta, which absorbed their delicate roasting juices. In the Veneto the dish was somewhat more elaborate: each little bird was wrapped in a cloak of pancetta and, after grilling, cradled in a square of firm polenta, inspiring the Milanese poet Carlo Porta to compose a sonnet to them. "As for the thrushes and blackbirds," he is said to have commented, "they were so fat, fresh and healthy it was a joy to look upon them and touch them. But the most intense joy was felt by the guests when they were brought piping hot to the table, draped as they were in bright clothing, with larduous majesty, sitting aloft polenta like Turks on a sofa!" So loved was this combination of songbirds and polenta, that plain polenta came to be known as *polenta e oseletti scapai*—polenta and the little birds that got away. Today, you hear tales of illicit feasts of songbirds and polenta, although restaurants generally substitute the somewhat larger quail for the forbidden delicacies.

be cooked with great success in the oven, an excellent technique when the oven is being used for other purposes, such as roasting chicken or vegetables. Then you can consolidate cooking and conserve resources. This technique is best when the polenta will be served immediately, rather than allowed to set up. Another technique preferred by many professional and casual cooks is to prepare polenta in a double boiler, a stovetop method that requires even less attention than cooking polenta over direct heat. Although much has been made recently of cooking polenta in a microwave oven, it is not a technique I recommend. It requires several stirrings throughout the twenty minutes or so it must cook—it takes much more time to open the door, remove the bowl, stir it, return it to the microwave, and reset the controls than it does to give a stovetop pot a quick stir—and the resulting flavor and texture are inferior to those of polenta cooked by other methods. However, a recipe is included here for those who must use a microwave. What is the best liquid in which to cook polenta? Some recipes recommend milk or a mixture of milk and water or stock. Some use stock only. With a few exceptions—certain soups, breads, and sweet puddings—I prefer to use water. A substantial portion of milk contributes an insipid, cloying quality to polenta (not to mention unnecessary calories from fat), and stocks frequently overwhelm the bright taste of corn. Save such ingredients for sauces, and cook basic polenta simply, with water and a bit of butter and cheese, which highlight rather than eclipse the corn flavor. Keep in mind that the quality of the water is essential—you want it to taste as pure and good as possible. If your tap water has off flavors, I recommend using spring water to prepare polenta. Also, if you have had a problem with lumps, use the cold water method (page 23) until you are more confident handling polenta. And keep in mind that the myth of cornmeal in a lump in the bottom of the pot, ruined because it was poured into the water too quickly, is just that—a myth. Certainly you must guard against lumps, but it is actually pretty difficult to ruin polenta. Polenta is both flexible and forgiving. It is impossible to give an exact cooking time because the qualities of specific cornmeals vary considerably, though you easily can have polenta on the table in thirty minutes or less. The freshness of the polenta, the type of corn from which it is made and the method by which it is ground, how fine or coarse the grain, its moisture content, where it has been stored, and in what container, all these influence how long polenta will take to become tender. Further, the degree of heat is crucial. If the heat is high, liquid will evaporate more quickly than it will be absorbed, requiring the addition of water and lengthier cooking. If initially you add more water than necessary, additional time will be necessary to evaporate excess liquid. I have rarely seen a bowl of polenta, no matter how thin and runny when it came off the stove, that failed to thicken eventually, though not necessarily enough to hold up to frying or grilling. Yet unlike pasta, you will not reach a point of no return when the polenta is overcooked and beyond

I arrive at Ristorante Ol Giopi e la Margi in Bergamo at noon on a warm spring morning, for a luncheon arranged by the Italian Trade Commission. I am escorted by the minister of agriculture, a local journalist, and Piero Ricci, head of the Knights of Polenta. The luncheon begins slowly, with sparkling wine and little appetizers: small balls of creamy polenta stuffed with cheese and fried; plump spoonfuls of polenta floating in warm cream; squares of polenta with luscious toppings. I taste polenta taragna, a traditional Bergamask preparation, for the first time; served in its own ramekin, it is bubbling hot from the oven and full of the rich, evocative flavors of buckwheat and sage, absolutely exquisite.

The meal unfolds magically as wine dissolves the language and cultural boundaries that separate us. Dish after enticing dish of polenta emerges from the kitchen, as the journalist translates with skill and finesse, though I must confess to merging with the meal's sensuality and disregarding the finer points of translation. The pivotal moment, the story I tell and retell, comes more than a dozen courses into the repast. Presented with polenta flanked by thin slices of meat in a dark gravy, I inquire as to what it is, exactly. The journalist speaks with the other guests, they gesture and shrug; finally, she confesses that she does not know the English word. All attempts at explanation are futile. Finally, Signor Ricci, the Grand Maestro of the *Ordine dei Cavalieri della Polenta,* a dapper, handsome man with beautiful silver hair, dressed in an elegant Italian suit, smiles and begins to bray: "Hee-haw, hee-haw, hee-haw," he cries, and we all dissolve in laughter. Polenta with donkey, another Bergamask tradition.

The *Ordine dei Cavalieri della Polenta*—The Order of the Knights of Polenta—was founded in Bergamo in northern Italy, not quite an hour's drive east of Milan, in November 1976. Its charter bids its members to "uphold, defend, and promote the use of polenta, and promote new ways to appreciate it, find the most suitable wines to enjoy with it, and to locate places where polenta is valued to the fullest." Members of the order are further encouraged to "reinforce feelings of sincerity, interest, and courtesy among themselves and to make gestures of solidarity whenever possible."

You could say that the Bergamask take polenta seriously, yet with a lighthearted flourish, their passion infused with fun and obvious pleasure. There is a council of seven members who on special occasions dress in full-length satin capes in Bergamo's official colors, red and gold. A small pin adorns each cape, and around each council member's neck, suspended by a red and gold ribbon, hangs a small wooden board, symbolizing the board onto which cooked polenta is poured. Both pin and board display the order's official coat of arms, a shield divided into four parts, a paiolo in the upper corner, a mound of golden polenta in the lower corner. Alternating sections are fields of gold, and the shield is topped with a green banner displaying the name of the order and a crown of corn in full bloom.

Meetings are held bimonthly, and each September, the Knights of Polenta join similar groups—the Knights of Osso Buco, of Funghi, of, presumably, Risotto—at an event called "At the Table with Friends." The traditional wines and foods of Lombardy, Piedmont, and Venice are presented in a grand feast, recipes are exchanged, and merriment prevails.

The *Ordine dei Cavalieri della Polenta* may be a contemporary organization, established to revive and preserve Bergamo's ancient heritage, yet it has illustrious ancestors. As early as the end of the 1700s, the Academy of the Polenta Eaters was founded in Pisa. A century later, Italian journalist Jacopo Caponi—known by his nom de plume, Folchetto—launched the Polenta Club in Paris, where the Brebant Restaurant served as a gathering place for the club's members, the Italian musicians, painters, writers, doctors, and financiers who had moved to Paris. There was an official song dedicated to the joys of polenta, and this group, too, had a coat of arms, a mosaic depicting golden polenta and a spit of grilled meat against a silver background, with the order's official motto, *Per Patria Prima Per Polenta Poi*—Allegiance First to Our Country, Then to Polenta.

rescue. Indeed, cooked polenta can be held over a pot of simmering water for quite a long time, where it will remain creamy until you need it. Preparing polenta, unlike, say, baking a cake or making an emulsified sauce, is an entirely intuitive process, with a considerable margin of error. It is essential to taste polenta—just as with pasta—as it nears doneness. The grains should be tender, there should be a distinct flavor of corn, and it should be the proper consistency, neither too thick nor too thin. Get to know polenta and learn to finesse it; it is really the only way to master its preparation. These three elements—flavor, texture, and consistency—are crucial. Regardless of the cooking method you use, you should be familiar enough with perfectly prepared polenta that a quick taste will tell you what is required, more or less liquid, more time on the heat, a different cornmeal. If the polenta does not taste like corn, the cornmeal is likely either old or of poor quality. There is nothing you can

PROMISCUOUS POLENTA

Polenta is nothing if not versatile; it accepts nearly any sauce, sweet or savory; creatures of the sea, land, and air all find it a welcoming abode; fruits and vegetables alike enjoy a luscious companionship with polenta. Acknowledging polenta's promiscuity, its eager willingness to couple with so diverse a group of culinary suitors, Italians often refer to polenta as "traviata," a somewhat out-of-character reference to Violetta, one of the main characters of the opera *La Traviata*. She was a courtesan, yes, but certainly not promiscuous.

do to correct this except store polenta correctly (page 12) and find a better source to begin with. Also, a strong stock may eclipse corn's delicate flavor. If the polenta tastes flat, it probably just needs a little salt, which will perk it up immediately. The individual grains should be tender yet retain a bit of texture. To serve soft and creamy polenta, the consistency should be similar to that of thick soup. The polenta should fall quickly from a spoon; Italians often refer to this creamy polenta as *polentina*. To serve soft polenta as a side dish with hearty sauces, poultry, and braised or grilled meats, you want the consistency to be slightly thicker but not stiff; it should hold its shape in a spoon. When it reaches this point, it should be served at once or held over a bath of simmering water. All polenta should rest off the heat for five minutes before serving. *N*early all polenta will thicken and be somewhat tender within fifteen or twenty minutes of cooking, though a longer time on the heat produces a creamier texture and more corn flavor. Cook your daily polenta as quickly as you need to, and when you're preparing it for a special occasion, give it the lengthy cooking that will develop its full flavors. Polenta that will be cut into shapes also needs lengthier cooking time (see specific recipes). *W*e all choose our concessions, the compromises we make daily so that they will cause us the least discomfort and provide the most pleasure we can squeeze into the fury of modern life. Some of us buy grated cheese and canned ragù, others bottled pesto, instant soups, frozen potatoes. Because of its reputation, polenta invites such compromises. Many excellent cooks find that instant polenta is perfectly acceptable, though purists blanch and call it blasphemy. Some cook polenta in the oven, while others rely on tubes of precooked polenta. This is true not only in America, which is ridiculed for its reliance on fast foods, but in Italy as well, where instant and precooked polenta are every bit as common as they are here, if not more so. *I*, too, have my compromises. I don't use instant polenta and I detest the precooked stuff, but I frequently pop my polenta into the oven rather than stir it on top of a stove. When I asked Grand Maestro Ricci (page 18) if this was an acceptable technique, his expression froze. "Absolutely not," he said adamantly, "not until after it has been cooked on the stove for an hour—and remember that an hour and a half is better. Then it can be sliced and baked, perhaps, but never *cooked* in the oven." Yet there you have my concession (with due apologies to my gracious Italian host); you must choose yours. Know the traditional techniques and all of the modern variations and select your favorite. The proof, as the saying goes, is in the pudding, in this case, the corn-meal pudding, the polenta.

soft polenta

Traditional Method

Serves 4 - 6

6 cups water

1 tablespoon kosher salt

1 cup coarse- or medium-ground polenta

½–1 teaspoon freshly ground black pepper

3 tablespoons butter

2 ounces Parmigiano-Reggiano, grated

This is the classic and most common technique for cooking polenta, and the one that should be used for larger quantities. The amounts can easily be increased to make larger quantities for a crowd.

IN A HEAVY pot, bring 3 cups water to a rolling boil. Have the remaining water simmering nearby. Add the salt and stir the water rapidly with a whisk, stirring in the same circular direction to create a vortex, into which pour the polenta in a thin, steady stream, stirring continuously all the while to prevent the formation of lumps. Continue to stir after all the polenta has been added, and lower the heat so that the mixture simmers slowly rather than boils. When the polenta begins to thicken, replace the whisk with a long-handled wooden spoon. Add 1 cup remaining water and continue to stir. Should you find lumps, use the back of the spoon to press them against the sides of the pot until they break up.

Continue to stir the polenta, being sure to reach down to the bottom of the pot, until it is thick and pulls away from the sides of the pot. Taste the polenta to be sure that the grains are tender; add more water as necessary. It will take 15 to 60 minutes, the longer time for certain types of cornmeal that simply do not become tender quickly.

During the last 5 minutes of cooking, stir in the pepper and butter, followed by the cheese. Remove from the heat. To serve immediately, pour onto a large platter or into a bowl or individual dishes. To make firm polenta, see page 29.

soft polenta

Cold Water Method

This technique is virtually foolproof when it comes to avoiding lumps. If you've had trouble in the past with lumps, use this method until you are more comfortable making polenta.

POUR 3 CUPS water into a large, heavy pot, add the salt, and stir in the polenta. Place the pot over high heat, stirring as the mixture comes to a boil. (Bring the remaining water to a boil in a separate container.) Lower the heat and simmer, stirring every few minutes until the mixture thickens, about 10 minutes. Add 1 cup additional water and continue to cook the polenta over low heat until it is tender. The polenta should be soft and creamy, without hard grains. Depending on the age and type of polenta, this will take 15 to 60 minutes; add more water as necessary. Stir regularly from the bottom of the pot so that the thickened polenta does not scorch. When the polenta is nearly ready, stir in the pepper and butter, followed by the cheese. Remove from the heat. To serve immediately, pour onto a large platter or into a bowl or individual dishes. To make firm polenta, see page 29.

Serves 4 – 6

6 cups boiling water

1 tablespoon kosher salt

½ teaspoon freshly ground black pepper

1 cup coarse-ground polenta

2 tablespoons butter

2 ounces Parmigiano-Reggiano, grated

soft polenta
Oven Method

Serves 4 – 6

This hands-off technique makes excellent polenta with very little effort or time on the cook's part. It results in creamy polenta with a very rich flavor.

1 quart water

1 tablespoon kosher salt

1/2–1 teaspoon freshly ground black pepper

1 cup coarse-ground polenta

2 tablespoons butter

PREHEAT THE OVEN to 350°F. In a 1 to 1½ quart container, stir together the water, salt, pepper, and polenta. Add the butter, cut in pieces. Place the container, uncovered, in the center of the top rack of the oven and bake for 40 minutes. Open the oven, pull out the rack, and stir the polenta. (This is also the time to add any additional ingredients such as cheese.) Close the oven and bake the polenta for an additional 10 minutes. Remove it from the oven, let rest for 5 minutes, and serve.

soft polenta
Double Boiler Method

Serves 4 – 6

This technique produces flavorful polenta without a great deal of hands-on attention. Use it when you must attend to other tasks in the kitchen.

6 cups boiling water

1 tablespoon kosher salt

1/2 teaspoon freshly ground black pepper

1 cup coarse-ground polenta

2 tablespoons butter

2 ounce Parmigiano-Reggiano, grated

FILL THE BOTTOM half of a double boiler with enough water that it will touch the upper half when it is inserted. Bring the water to a boil, reduce the heat, and keep the water at a simmer.

Place 4 cups boiling water in the top portion of the double boiler, stir in the salt, pepper, and polenta, and set it in the bottom half of the double boiler. Bring the water and polenta back to a boil, cover very tightly, and simmer over medium-low heat until the polenta is soft and tender. Every 20 minutes or so, remove the lid and stir the polenta, using a long-handled wooden spoon. Continue this process, adding additional water as necessary, until the polenta is thick, tender, and pulls away from the sides of the pot, about 1½ hours. Add the butter and cheese during the last 10 minutes of cooking. When it is done, remove the polenta from the heat, pour onto a large platter or into a bowl or individual dishes, and serve immediately.

soft polenta
Microwave Method

*Use this method when a microwave oven is the only source available
to you. And be aware that polenta cooked by this method will set
up firm quickly as it cools.*

IN A LARGE glass bowl, combine the water, polenta, salt, and pepper, and
place in the center of the microwave oven. Cook at full power for 5 minutes,
remove from the microwave, stir, and return for another 5 minutes at full
power. Repeat and, this time, stir in the butter before returning the polenta to
the oven. Cook a fourth time for 5 minutes, remove from the oven, and taste
(carefully, it will be quite hot). If the polenta is not quite tender, stir in an
additional $1/2$ cup boiling water and return to the oven for 3 minutes at full
power. Remove from the oven and serve immediately.

Serves 4 – 6

$4^{1}/_{2}$ cups boiling water

**1 cup coarse-ground
polenta**

**2 teaspoons kosher
salt**

**$1/2$–1 teaspoon freshly
ground black pepper**

1 tablespoon butter

polenta nera

*This traditional recipe produces a firm, dense porridge the color of a bleak
winter sky and full of deep, earthy flavors. Serve it with winter vegetables
such as baked squash, sautéed chard, and wild mushroom fricasee.*

IN A HEAVY, medium saucepan, mix together the buckwheat flour, stock,
and salt. Set over medium heat and stir continuously until the mixture comes
to a boil. Reduce the heat to low and simmer for 20 minutes, stirring regularly.
Add the butter and cheese, stir until well incorporated, and remove from the
heat. Pour the polenta nera into a baking dish or onto a baking sheet with
sides (brush the container lightly with olive oil), let cool, cover with plastic
wrap or wax paper, and refrigerate until ready to use.

Serves 4 – 6

1 cup buckwheat flour

3 cups chicken stock

1 teaspoon kosher salt

1 tablespoon butter

**$1/2$ ounce Parmigiano-
Reggiano, grated**

flavored polenta

THERE ARE SEVERAL ways to add flavor to polenta, the most common being when cheese, sauce, or a stew is added as a topping; the foods served with polenta contribute the flavors. But flavor nuances can be introduced directly into the polenta while it cooks or as soon as it is done, before a sauce or topping is added. (This is a convenient way to give another dimension to polenta.) The basic rule to follow when adding seasonings directly to polenta is not to overwhelm it but rather to add ingredients in amounts that that will blend well and highlight the corn's natural qualities. In the end, polenta should still taste like corn. Salt, butter, and cheese are almost always essential; without salt and a bit of flavorful fat, polenta tastes flat. Garlic adds a pleasant dimension, as do sautéed onions, sliced olives, fresh herbs, certain spices, lemon zest, hot peppers and chiles, and tomato paste, which also gives the polenta a pleasing rosy hue.

To flavor polenta, begin with the one of the basic recipes, either the Traditional Method (page 22), the Cold Water Method (page 23), or the Double Boiler Method (page 24), which produce the best results. Prepare the flavoring ingredients, add them as described below, and serve the polenta as a side dish or with toppings that resonate with the flavor of the polenta.

Lemon Zest   Add 1 tablespoon minced lemon zest to the polenta just before removing it from the stove.

Sun-dried Tomatoes   Add ¼ cup dried tomato bits (see Resources, page 133) to the boiling water before adding the dry polenta.

Tomato Paste   Stir 2 tablespoons double-concentrated tomato paste and 2 teaspoons dried oregano into the boiling water before adding the dry polenta. After adding the butter and cheese near the end of cooking, taste and correct the seasoning with additional salt and pepper, if necessary.

Fresh Herbs   Toss together 2 tablespoons minced Italian parsley, 1 tablespoon minced basil, 1 teaspoon minced oregano, 1 teaspoon minced marjoram, and ½ teaspoon minced rosemary. Place in a small saucepan, add ½ cup heavy cream, set over medium heat, and just heat through. Let steep until the polenta is nearly finished cooking; add the herbs and cream to the polenta just before removing it from the stove, stirring well to distribute the flavors evenly.

Fresh Sage and Shallots Peel and mince 3 shallots and sauté in 1 tablespoon butter until soft and fragrant. Add 2 tablespoons minced fresh sage, stir, and remove from the heat. Add to the polenta with the pepper, butter, and cheese.

Walnuts and Parsley Toss together 3/4 cup coarsely chopped toasted walnuts, 2 tablespoons minced fresh Italian parsley, and 2 teaspoons minced fresh garlic. Add to the polenta with a full teaspoon of pepper, the butter, and the cheese.

Olives and Herbs Toss together 3/4 cup pitted sliced olives (for best results use a combination of Niçoise, Picholine, and Kalamata olives), 1 teaspoon minced fresh basil, and 1 teaspoon minced fresh oregano. Add to the polenta with the pepper, butter, and cheese.

Onions and Curry Mince a small yellow onion and sauté it in 1 tablespoon butter until soft and fragrant. Add 2 teaspoons curry powder, 1 teaspoon toasted cumin seeds or 1/2 teaspoon ground cumin, 1/2 teaspoon ground turmeric, and a pinch of cayenne pepper, stir, and sauté for an additional 2 minutes. Add to the boiling water before adding the dry polenta. Instead of additional butter and cheese, stir 3/4 cup unflavored yogurt into the polenta. When it is finished cooking, taste and season with additional salt, pepper, and cayenne to taste.

Chiles and Cilantro Sauté 3 garlic cloves in 2 tablespoons butter or olive oil. Add 1 to 3 minced serrano or jalapeño chiles (depending on the heat) and sauté until soft. Replace the Parmigiano with either Mexican *queso fresca* or Monterey Jack, and increase the amount to 3 ounces. Add the sautéed peppers with the cheese, remove the polenta from the heat, and stir in 1/4 cup cilantro leaves.

polenta shapes

There are three basic techniques for making polenta shapes: pour the polenta directly into large or individual molds that have been brushed with olive oil or rinsed with cold water and left wet (to ensure that the polenta slips out easily); pour the polenta onto a sheet pan lined with wax paper, let it set up for about 20 minutes, and then cut the desired shapes using a sharp knife or a pastry or cookie cutter; or let the polenta cool for 10 to 15 minutes after cooking, spoon it into a pastry bag fitted with a large star or circular tip, and pipe individual stars of polenta (page 38) onto a sheet of wax paper and allow them to set up before serving.

POLENTA LASAGNA

Although there are many who will disagree with me, I believe that polenta lasagna is mostly a word game that borrows an appealing term but does not transform it. It is applied to various layered polentas, a technique that existed long before anyone decided to term it "lasagna." Several of the dishes in this book could be referred to in this manner; the polenta loaf with mushrooms, for example, or polenta with *ragù*, could be called polenta lasagna, if I were so inclined.

I've seen recipes that call for polenta to be set up in a sheet pan, unmolded onto a work surface, and then sliced lengthwise with a long, thin knife. It is then layered with traditional or innovative sauces and other ingredients. In testing recipes for this book, I found that layering the polenta while it is still warm and creamy is not only easier but produces a better mingling of flavors and textures. And so you will not find any recipes here with "lasagna" in their titles. Forgive me if I seem pedantic, but this is my best advice.

firm polenta for fried, grilled, and broiled polenta

You also can make polenta shapes from flavored polenta (pages 26–27) and adjust the quantities accordingly. If you plan on piping the polenta through a pastry bag, be certain all ingredients are small enough to fit through the tip.

IN A LARGE heavy pot, bring the water to a boil, add the salt, and stir in the polenta. Stir continuously until the polenta thickens, about 15 minutes, lower the heat, and continue to cook, stirring regularly, until the polenta is tender, 30 to 60 minutes. During the last 5 minutes of cooking, stir in the pepper and butter, followed by the cheese. Remove from the heat and let rest for 10 minutes. Pour onto a baking sheet, $17^{1}/_{4} \times 12^{1}/_{4}$ inches (see Note), that has been lined with wax or parchment paper and brushed lightly with olive oil. Use a rubber spatula dipped in cold water to spread the polenta evenly. Brush a second sheet of wax paper or parchment paper with olive oil, place it, oiled side down, on top of the hot polenta. Let cool at room temperature for 20 minutes and then refrigerate it for at least 1 hour before cutting into shapes. If you refrigerate the polenta for longer than 2 hours, wrap it tightly in plastic (in addition to topping it with wax or parchment paper).

Individual Molds: While the polenta is cooling, prepare small individual molds by rubbing the insides with a thin coating of olive oil. Fill each mold with the polenta and allow it to sit at room temperature until firm. Depending on the size of the mold, this will take 20 to 60 minutes. To serve, invert the mold over a serving plate. The polenta should slip out easily. If it does not, use the tip of a knife around the edge to coax it out. Individual molds, covered, can be refrigerated and reheated before serving.

Note: This is the standard size of a commercial half-sheet pan; available in restaurant supply stores and better cookware stores.

Makes 64 2-inch squares or circles; 20 3-inch squares or circles; or 40 triangles

12 cups water

4 tablespoons kosher salt

$^{1}/_{2}$–1 teaspoon freshly ground black pepper

3 cups coarse-ground polenta

4 ounces (1 stick) butter, cut into pieces

2$^{1}/_{2}$ ounces Parmigiano-Reggiano, grated

---

frying

Polenta will keep its shape better if it is cold when fried, so refrigerate polenta shapes, covered, for 1 hour or more before cooking. Dredging the polenta in flour or fine cornmeal will contribute a more finished appearance and a better texture to the outside. The shapes must be dipped in egg first, however, so that the flour or cornmeal will adhere to the surface. This step can be omitted if you like and the polenta fried directly in the olive oil.

Polenta Shapes (page 28), cut into shape of choice

Olive oil

1–2 eggs, beaten (optional)

All-purpose flour or finely ground cornmeal (optional)

POUR A SMALL amount of olive oil into a large, even-surfaced, heavy skillet and place it over medium heat. Pour the egg, if using, into a low bowl or plate; add about 1/4 cup flour to a second plate. Dip the polenta shapes first in the egg, turning to coat both sides, then dredge them in the flour or cornmeal, patting to shake off excess flour. Place the polenta in the frying pan, repeat until the pan is full, but not crowded. Work in batches, adding more olive oil as necessary and allowing it to heat up before adding more polenta shapes. Fry the shapes until they begin to take on a little color, turn and fry the other side until golden. Total cooking time should be about 8 minutes. Transfer the polenta shapes to absorbent paper, then to a serving platter or individual plates before adding toppings or other accompaniments.

broiling

This is a simple, nearly foolproof method of toasting polenta shapes,
particularly effective if you have an oven with a good broiler.

HAVE THE POLENTA shapes cold before you begin. Brush a baking sheet
with a light coating of olive oil, arrange the polenta shapes on the sheet, and
place under a preheated broiler until they just begin to color. Remove from
the broiler, turn them to the other side, and broil until golden. Remove and
transfer to a serving platter or individual plates before adding toppings or
other accompaniments.

Olive oil

Polenta Shapes (page 28), cut into shape of choice

grilling

Grilling polenta is somewhat trickier than it sounds. First, when preparing
the polenta, you should cover the surface with wax or parchment paper
brushed with olive oil to prevent the formation of a thin crust that may come
off during grilling. Next, it is essential that the grill surface be very clean so
that the polenta does not stick to it. Finally, if you have not had success
grilling polenta in the past—if it falls apart or sticks to the grill—consider
dredging it in egg and flour, as described in the Frying technique on page 30,
before grilling. Stovetop grills sometimes work better than charcoal grills.

HAVE THE POLENTA shapes cold before you begin. Place each piece of
polenta on a medium-hot grill for about 3 minutes, until it is well marked and
hot. Turn and grill until well marked on the other side. When you turn the
polenta, use a good spatula with straight, sharp sides. Hold the side of the
spatula next to the polenta and scrape it off the grill and onto the spatula with
a sharp, slightly downward motion. Turn a second time on each side, rotating
the polenta to score it in both directions. Transfer to a serving platter or individual plates before adding toppings or other accompaniments.

Firm Polenta for Fried, Grilled, and Broiled Polenta (page 29), cut into shape of choice

appetizers

polenta crostini

Firm Polenta for Fried, Grilled, and Broiled Polenta (page 29)

Flavored Polenta (pages 26–27), prepared for shapes (page 28)

One or more toppings (recipes follow)

Small squares, triangles, or circles of polenta make an ideal canvas for a savory topping, perfect as part of a buffet, to be passed as appetizers or served as a first course. Polenta crostini have a long history in Italy, and today Italian restaurants frequently offer a selection to begin a meal. You can do the same with just a little advance planning. Choose a single topping or select three or four with flavors and textures that complement each other. Polenta crostini are best when fried, broiled, or grilled, but you can also serve them at room temperature or heat them in the oven before adding toppings.

TO SERVE POLENTA shapes as appetizers, cut them into small shapes with a knife or decorative cookie cutter of your choice. Broil, grill, or fry them until they are hot and just beginning to turn golden brown. Transfer them from the heat to decorative trays, add toppings, and serve immediately. To serve as a first course, once the polenta shapes are hot, arrange several on individual serving plates. Add the toppings and serve immediately.

SIMPLE TOPPINGS

Add the following toppings to the polenta shapes after they have been fried, grilled, or broiled. Do not overwhelm them with too much of any topping.

Gorgonzola and Fresh Rosemary Add about ½ teaspoon cheese and 2 to 3 minced rosemary needles to each piece of polenta.

Fresh Chèvre and Chives Slice or crumble fresh chèvre, top each piece of polenta with a small portion and a few snipped chives.

Soppressata Cut thin slices of soppressata or other Italian salami in half and place on each piece of hot polenta.

Prosciutto Cut thin slices of prosciutto into strips twice as long as the pieces of polenta. Gather each strip of prosciutto like a loose ribbon and place it on top of a piece of hot polenta. Serve plain or with a tiny dollop of Dijon mustard.

Chutney and Cilantro Leaves Add a small spoonful of your favorite chutney to each piece of hot polenta and top with 1 or 2 cilantro leaves.

Corn Salsa Top each piece with 1 teaspoon Corn Salsa (page 83).

Shredded Arugula Rinse and dry 1 bunch young arugula leaves. Remove the stems and stack the leaves. Cut them into *very* thin strips, cutting crosswise not lengthwise. Toss with a very small amount of extra virgin olive oil, season with kosher salt and freshly ground black pepper, and top each piece of polenta with some of the shredded mixture.

Roasted Sweet Peppers Cut 1 yellow and 1 red roasted sweet pepper into julienne strips and toss with a minced anchovy and 1 or 2 tablespoons red wine vinegar. Top each piece with a small amount of the mixture.

Tapenade and Chèvre Chop 1¼ cups Niçoise olives, pitted, and ¼ cup Picholine olives, pitted, with a sharp knife (not in a food processor) and combine them with 2 minced salt-cured anchovies, 1 minced garlic clove, and 1 tablespoon minced Italian parsley. Stir in ½ cup olive oil. Prepare the polenta shapes, and top each hot piece with a bit of chèvre and a small spoonful of tapenade. Serve immediately.

Pesto Place 3 cups packed basil leaves and 8 garlic cloves in a food processor and pulse until both are finely chopped. Add ¾ cup extra virgin olive oil and pulse until not quite smooth. Transfer the mixture to a medium bowl and stir in 5 tablespoons softened butter, followed by ¾ cup (about 3 ounces) freshly grated imported Parmigiano-Reggiano, ¼ cup (about 1 ounce) freshly grated Pecorino-Romano, and ½ cup pine nuts. Taste the pesto and add kosher salt if necessary. Heat the polenta shapes and top each with a small spoonful of pesto. Leftover pesto may be stored in the refrigerator in an airtight container for up to 1 week.

Dried Tomato Pesto Place ½ cup dried tomato bits in a small container and add enough boiling water to just cover them. Let them cool to room temperature. Place ¾ cup basil leaves, ¼ cup parsley leaves, 4 to 6 garlic cloves, ½ teaspoon finely minced lemon zest, 1 tablespoon softened butter, and 1 teaspoon kosher salt in a food processor and pulse until the ingredients form a relatively smooth mixture. Add the cooled tomato bits and ⅓ cup Parmigiano-Reggiano and pulse again 2 or 3 times. Add ⅓ to ½ cup extra virgin olive oil, using the full amount for a slightly looser sauce. Transfer the pesto to a bowl or jar. Heat the polenta shapes, top each with a small spoonful of the pesto, garnish with a leaf of basil or parsley, and serve immediately. Leftover pesto may be stored in a covered jar in the refrigerator for up to 2 weeks.

Pistada (Emilian Pesto)

In her book *Italy in Small Bites* (Morrow, 1993), Carol Field offers a succulent condiment based on Italy's *lardo,* made from chunks of choice pork back fat layered with spices and preserved in marble basins rubbed with garlic. This recipe, inspired by hers, offers a compromise; it's wonderful served atop squares of fried polenta.

Place 6 to 8 garlic cloves in a food processor fitted with a steel blade. Pulse several times to chop the garlic, open the container, use a rubber spatula to scrape the garlic from the sides, close, and pulse again. Add 6 ounces pancetta, white part only, coarsely chopped, and pulse to make a smooth paste. Add $^1/_2$ cup minced fresh parsley, $^1/_2$ teaspoon minced rosemary, a pinch of salt, and freshly ground black pepper, and process until all of the ingredients are smoothly blended. Transfer to a small bowl. Fry the polenta shapes and top each with a small amount of the pistada.

COOKED TOPPINGS

Grilled and Sliced Sausages

Grill sausages of choice—they should be robustly flavored—drain them of excess fat, slice them $^1/_4$ inch thick, and top each piece of polenta with 1 round.

Ragù

Top each piece of polenta with a small spoonful of hot ragù (page 98), or spoon the sauce onto a small plate and set hot polenta atop the sauce.

Salt Cod in Cream

Top each piece of polenta with a small spoonful of hot salt cod (page 86).

Wild Mushroom Ragoût

In a small sauté pan, melt 2 tablespoons unsalted butter. When it is foamy, add 1 minced medium shallot, sauté for 5 minutes, add 2 minced garlic cloves, and sauté for an additional 2 minutes. Add $^1/_4$ pound wild or cultivated specialty mushrooms, broken into medium pieces, and $^1/_2$ cup white wine. Cover the pan and simmer until the mushrooms are wilted, 5 to 7 minutes. Remove the lid, and simmer until the white wine is nearly completely evaporated. Remove from the heat, add 1 tablespoon minced Italian parsley, salt, and freshly ground black pepper to taste. Set aside.

Serve with broiled or grilled polenta triangles. Spoon the mushrooms over the triangles, garnish with sprigs of Italian parsley, and serve immediately.

Chicken Livers with Sage Heat 2 tablespoons olive oil in a small frying pan. Add 1 minced shallot, sauté for 5 minutes, add the 2 minced garlic cloves, and sauté for another 2 minutes. Add ½ pound chicken livers, trimmed of fat and cut into small pieces, and sauté quickly, agitating the pan to cook the livers thoroughly but quickly. Add pinch ground cloves, 1 teaspoon minced sage leaves, salt, and freshly ground black pepper. Remove from the heat when the livers are just barely done. Taste and correct the seasonings. Serve atop hot polenta shapes and garnish each portion with a small sage leaf.

Walnut Sauce Prepare the polenta shapes. In a small bowl, combine 6 tablespoons softened butter, 6 tablespoons grated Parmigiano-Reggiano, 6 tablespoons walnut pieces, toasted and finely chopped, 1 tablespoon finely minced Italian parsley, 1 teaspoon kosher salt, and 1 teaspoon freshly ground black pepper. Stir in 5 tablespoons heavy cream. When the polenta shapes are hot, top each with a small spoonful of walnut sauce.

White Bean Puree Heat 3 tablespoons olive oil in a small saucepan and sauté ½ small yellow onion, minced, over medium heat until it is soft and fragrant, about 15 minutes. Add 3 minced garlic cloves, sauté for 2 minutes, and add 1 cup cooked, drained cannellini beans. With a fork mash the beans into a smooth puree as they cook, stirring constantly so they do not scorch. If the mixture seems a little dry, add a small amount of water. Stir in 2 teaspoons minced sage and 2 ounces grated Parmigiano-Reggiano, remove from the heat, taste, and season with salt and freshly ground black pepper. Place a small spoonful of the puree on each piece of hot polenta and drizzle with a small amount of extra virgin olive oil.

Pears and Gorgonzola Prepare the polenta shapes. Peel and score 2 firm, ripe pears. Slice pears into ⅛-inch pieces. In a medium saucepan, melt 1 tablespoon butter and sauté several pear slices until they are tender and golden. Continue until all the pear slices have been cooked. Top each broiled or grilled polenta shape with a slice of pear and a small amount of Gorgonzola. Serve immediately.

polenta stars

This is a slightly more elegant and complex version of polenta shapes and is excellent for serving a crowd. First, the polenta is flavored, and then it is passed through a pastry bag fitted with a star tip. It takes a little time to master the technique, but your efforts are rewarded with a pretty appetizer that can be made in advance. Before you begin, be sure to have a good pastry bag fitted with a large star tip. You can use this technique with most flavored polentas (pages 26–27); polenta stars make an excellent addition to an antipasto platter.

4 cups water

1 teaspoon kosher salt

$\frac{1}{4}$ cup dried tomato bits

1 cup polenta

3 tablespoons butter

3 garlic cloves, pressed

2 ounces Gorgonzola

3 ounces Parmigiano-Reggiano, grated

2 ounces Pecorino-Romano, grated

Pesto (page 35) or Dried Tomato Pesto (page 35)

BRING THE WATER and salt to a boil, and stir in the dried tomato bits. Slowly pour in the polenta, whisking continuously in the same direction to discourage the formation of lumps. When all of the polenta has been incorporated, lower the heat and simmer for 20 to 25 minutes, stirring regularly and adding additional water if necessary. When the polenta has thickened, stir in the butter and garlic. Break up the Gorgonzola and add it, along with the other cheeses, to the polenta. Stir well, taste, and if the polenta is sufficiently tender, remove it from the heat. Let it rest until it cools just slightly but does not become firm, or about 10 minutes; stir it every few minutes.

To make the polenta stars, line a baking sheet with wax paper and brush the wax paper with olive oil. Ladle the polenta into the pastry bag and wrap a towel around the bag to protect your hands from the heat. Squeeze stars of polenta onto the wax paper—about 2 teaspoons to each star—by holding the pastry bag steady and pointing downward. Leave about $\frac{1}{2}$ inch between stars. Let the stars set up for at least 15 minutes before serving. Use a metal spatula to transfer the stars to a plate and top each star with about $\frac{1}{4}$ teaspoon pesto.

antipasto of polenta, salami, sardines, and shallots

This recipe is one of more than a dozen I was served during my grand polenta feast in Bergamo. In Italian it is called Margherita di Polenta, *which refers to the flower we call an African daisy. With its center of yellow polenta and petals of salami, flanked by fragrant shallots and silvery sardines, this appetizer is both beautiful and delicious.*

Serves 4 – 6

LET THE POLENTA set up either in a sheet pan or in individual molds, such as small ramekins or muffin tins brushed with olive oil. Place the sardines in a low bowl, pour the red wine vinegar over them, and set aside. In a small sauté pan, heat a small amount of olive oil, add the shallots, and sauté until they just begin to color. Add the white wine, reduce the heat, cover the pan, and simmer until the shallots are just tender.

To arrange the antipasto, place a round of polenta on each of 6 serving plates. Arrange the salami around each polenta round, creating a petal effect. Add 4 sardines and 2 pieces of shallot to each plate, season the shallots with a little salt and pepper, garnish with a sprig of Italian parsley, and serve.

¹/₂ recipe Soft Polenta (page 22)

1 can sardines packed in olive oil, drained

3 tablespoons red wine vinegar

Olive oil

6 shallots, cut in half

¹/₃ cup dry white wine

24 thin slices (about 3 ounces) Italian salami, such as soppressata, cut in half

Kosher salt and black pepper in a mill

Sprigs of Italian parsley, for garnish

breads

polenta grissini

Grissini, or breadsticks, are another thing entirely from the anemic dry pencils we find here in both markets and restaurants. There are numerous versions in Italy, yet none that I know of made with polenta. When testing recipes for this book, we liked the pizza crust so much that it inspired us to use it to make these. They are best eaten within a day of baking, but can be wrapped and stored in the refrigerator for up to 2 days.

2 teaspoons dry yeast

$1/4$ cup warm water

$1^2/3$ cups all-purpose flour

1 cup fine-ground yellow polenta

1 tablespoon sugar

3 teaspoons kosher salt

$3/4$ cup water, room temperature

1 egg white mixed with 1 tablespoon water

IN A SMALL bowl, mix together the yeast and warm water, and let rest for 10 minutes. Meanwhile, combine the flour, polenta, sugar, and 2 teaspoons salt. Stir the yeast into the flour mixture, add the water, and stir quickly until the mixture comes together as dough. Turn out onto a floured work surface and knead for 5 to 7 minutes until the dough is smooth and somewhat velvety. Place in an oiled bowl, cover, and let rise in a warm place until double, about 2 hours.

Punch down, cut the dough into 12 equal pieces, and then roll each piece between the palms of your hands into a stick approximately 10 inches long. If your oven has a baking stone, set each piece of dough on a baking sheet without sides that has been sprinkled heavily with polenta. If you do not have a baking stone, any baking sheet that will hold all the grissini will do. Brush the grissini with the egg wash and sprinkle with the remaining salt. Cover and let rise again until double, about 1 hour.

To bake, carefully slide the grissini off the baking sheet and onto the baking stone in an oven preheated to 375°F. Alternately, place the baking sheet with the grissini into the preheated oven. Bake for 12 to 15 minutes until the grissini have just begun to color. Remove from the oven and transfer each grissini to a cooling rack.

polenta pizza with brie and red grapes

Of all the various toppings we tried with this crust, this was by far everyone's favorite. There is a tradition of sweet focaccia, an Italian flat bread not exactly the same, yet not entirely unlike pizza, and one version calls for grapes. Here, in this polenta version, mild and creamy Brie complements the sweet grapes, and toasted walnuts provide additional flavor and texture.

Makes one 10-inch pizza

IN A MEDIUM mixing bowl, combine the yeast with ¼ cup warm water and let sit for 10 minutes. Stir in the remaining water, olive oil, and salt, and then mix in the flour and polenta. Turn out the soft dough onto a floured work surface and knead for 7 minutes. Place the dough in a large, oiled bowl, cover, and let rise in a warm place until double, about 1½ hours. Punch down, pat, or roll into a 10-inch circle, place on a pizza paddle, cover, and let rise for 1 hour.

Brush the dough with the melted butter and arrange the slices of Brie over the surface. Scatter the grapes and walnuts over the Brie, and then sprinkle the sugar over all. Transfer the pizza to a baking stone in an oven preheated to 450°F and bake for 12 to 15 minutes until the edges of the crust just begin to turn golden. Remove from the oven, let cool for 5 minutes, cut into 8 slices, and serve immediately.

- 2 teaspoons yeast
- ⅞ cup warm water
- 2 tablespoons olive oil
- 1 teaspoon kosher salt
- 1½ cups all-purpose flour
- ¾ cup fine-ground polenta
- 2 teaspoons unsalted butter, melted
- 4 ounces Brie, cut into thin slices
- 1 cup Red Flame grapes (or other seedless red grape), sliced in half
- ¼ cup walnut pieces, toasted
- 2 teaspoons turbinado sugar

soppressata, pepper, and gorgonzola polenta pizza

Brush the dough with olive oil instead of butter, cover the surface of the pizza with the soppressata; spread the roasted peppers over the top, then scatter the cheese over the meat and peppers and bake.

(continued)

- 2 tablespoons extra virgin olive oil
- 12–16 slices soppressata
- ¾ cup roasted sweet peppers, cut into julienne
- 3 ounces Gorgonzola or fresh chèvre

2 tablespoons extra virgin olive oil

4 ounces fresh mozzarella, sliced

Handful basil leaves

2 teaspoons minced garlic

3–4 small or medium ripe tomatoes, cored and sliced crosswise

Kosher salt and black pepper in a mill

Makes 4

8 3-inch squares or triangles of Firm Polenta (page 29), no more than ¹/₂ inch thick

4 thin slices prosciutto

2 ounces Gorgonzola

8 sage leaves

Olive oil

1 egg, lightly beaten

¹/₄ cup all-purpose flour

polenta pizza margherita

Brush the dough with olive oil instead of butter, cover the surface with the sliced mozzarella; arrange the basil leaves on top, then scatter the garlic over the basil. Top with the tomatoes. Sprinkle with salt and pepper.

polenta sandwiches with prosciutto, gorgonzola, and sage

You can make these appealing little sandwiches with virtually any sliced Italian meat—pancetta that has been sliced and fried, for example, or soppressata and other Italian salamis—and cheese of your preference. This makes an excellent antipasto that is simple to prepare when you have leftover polenta.

ARRANGE THE SQUARES or triangles of polenta on a work surface. Place 1 slice of prosciutto on each of 4 pieces of polenta, folding the prosciutto so it fits and does not hang over the edges of the polenta. Top with ¹/₂ ounce Gorgonzola and then add 2 sage leaves to each polenta piece. Top each with one of the remaining pieces of polenta.

Heat some olive oil in a heavy skillet over medium heat, dip the sandwiches, one by one, in the egg, turning to coat them thoroughly, and then dredge them in flour. Fry the sandwiches until fairly crispy on all sides. Set on a serving platter and serve immediately.

an unusual
corn bread

This bread, based on American ingredients and European techniques, may appear more difficult than it really is. Although it requires several hours of fermentation, actual hands-on work is minimal. If you begin by making the poolish in the evening and letting it ferment through the night, you can have bread by the next afternoon. Craig Ponsford, the baker and co-owner of Artisan Bakers in Sonoma County, developed this recipe as one of several traditional breads he baked in the 1996 Coupe de Monde du Boulangerie (World Cup of Baking) in Paris. His efforts secured the top prize for the U.S.A. Team, a first for the United States, which competed with teams from nine other countries.

TO MAKE THE poolish, mix together the flour, water, and yeast in a medium mixing bowl until well blended. Cover loosely and let ferment in a warm place (70 to 75°F) for 15 hours; overnight is ideal.

To make the pre-fermented dough, mix together the flour, water, salt, and yeast in a medium bowl until well blended, cover lightly, set aside, and let rise at 70 to 75°F for 3 hours.

To prepare the final dough, place 1¼ cups water and the polenta in a small saucepan. Bring to a boil and simmer for 3 to 4 minutes to soften the grain. Rinse in cool water, drain thoroughly, and cool completely. Combine the flours, cooled polenta, remaining water, poolish, and pre-fermented dough in the container of an electric mixer fitted with a paddle attachment. Mix until well blended, add the yeast and then the salt, mixing briefly after each addition. Mix at slow speed for 4 minutes and then at high speed for 4 minutes. The dough should be soft and pull away from the sides of the bowl. Place the dough in a large, clean bowl brushed with olive oil, cover with a damp towel, set it in a warm place (approximately 70 to 75°F). Let rise for 1 hour, punch down, and let rise for another hour.

To shape, divide the dough into two pieces and shape into rounds. Let rest for 20 minutes, flatten slightly, and then shape into triangles by folding the

Makes 2 loaves

Poolish
4 ounces all-purpose flour

1 cup water

¼ teaspoon yeast

Pre-fermented dough
9½ ounces all-purpose flour

⅞ cup warm (about 75°F) water

½ teaspoon kosher salt

½ teaspoon yeast

Final Dough

2 cups water

1¹⁄₂ ounces coarse-ground polenta

4 ounces (1 cup) all-purpose flour

8¹⁄₂ ounces (2 cups plus 2 tablespoons) corn flour

1¹⁄₂ teaspoons dried yeast (or ¹⁄₄ ounce cake yeast)

1 tablespoon kosher salt

Olive oil

dough into the center on three sides. Turn and let rise, seam side down, for 1 hour.

During the last rise, preheat the oven and baking tiles or pizza stone to 400°F.

Carefully transfer the dough to the oven. Reduce the heat to 375°F, spritz the oven several times (using a spray bottle) with water to create steam, close the door, and bake for approximately 20 minutes. Open the oven door slightly and bake for an additional 10 minutes until the crust is golden brown. Remove from the oven and cool on a baking rack.

breakfast polenta

polenta and milk

Serves 4

"Cold polenta from the day before," my Italian recipe reads, "and as much hot milk as needed." I came away from my polenta feast at Ristorante Ol Giopi e la Margi in Bergamo with a handful of enticing recipes written, of course, in Italian. Between the beautiful accompanying photographs, my rather rough culinary Italian, and the help of a couple of friends, I deciphered nearly all the details. There are two versions of this simple and common preparation of polenta, one using leftover polenta and one with polenta cooked on the spot. Either is just the thing on a cold morning.

Soft Polenta (page 22), not too creamy, or a comparable amount of leftover polenta

3 cups milk, approximately

IF USING LEFTOVER polenta, cut it in large cubes and divide it among 4 serving bowls. Bring the milk to a boil, remove it from the heat, and pour it over each portion of polenta. Serve immediately.

If using freshly made polenta, pour a small amount of cold milk into each of 4 bowls. Use a teaspoon to form rounds of polenta, divide them among the bowls, pour some of the remaining milk over each portion, and serve immediately.

baked eggs and polenta

Serves 4

This dish, perfect for a winter brunch, also can be prepared with fried or poached eggs, if you prefer. Simply prepare the eggs to your liking and set them atop bowls of creamy polenta.

Soft Polenta (page 22)

4–6 large eggs

Kosher salt and black pepper in a mill

Parmigiano-Reggiano, grated (optional)

Tabasco sauce, hot sauce, or salsa (optional)

PREPARE CREAMY POLENTA and when it is done, divide it among ovenproof bowls. Break an egg over each serving and place the bowls in a 375°F oven until the eggs are set but the yolks are still soft, about 5 minutes. Remove from the oven, season with salt and pepper, top with grated cheese or hot sauce or salsa on the side. Serve immediately.

eggs poached in tomato sauce with grilled polenta

Here's a sensational breakfast dish, rich and full of intriguing contrasts of flavor and texture, with the polenta triangles serving as a sort of toast to soak up the aromatic sauce. It is best when made with authentic ranch eggs; if you do not have a source, look for one at a farmers' market near you.

Serves 4

HEAT THE OLIVE oil in a large, heavy frying pan and sauté the onion until it is fragrant and tender, about 15 minutes. Add the chicken stock and reduce over medium heat by one half. Stir in the tomato sauce, lower the heat, and simmer for 30 minutes. Taste the sauce, and if it is particularly acidic, add a pinch of sugar. Stir in the red pepper flakes and vinegar, and season to taste with salt and several turns of black pepper. The sauce can be made a day or two in advance.

To complete the dish, bring the sauce to a simmer in a large, wide pan. When the sauce is hot, gently break one egg onto a saucer and then slide it into the sauce. Repeat with the remaining eggs, spacing them around the outer edge so as not to crowd them. Spoon a little sauce over the top of each egg, cover the pan, and simmer briefly until the eggs are just set but the yolks still soft.

While the eggs cook, quickly fry, grill, or broil the polenta triangles and place a triangle on each of 4 warmed serving plates. Using a large, slotted spoon, top each polenta triangle with an egg. Divide the sauce among the 4 servings and top each with a sprinkling of parsley and a couple of turns of black pepper. Serve immediately.

2 tablespoons olive oil

1 small red onion, diced

1 cup chicken stock

2 cups tomato sauce (fresh, home canned, or commercial)

Pinch granulated sugar (optional)

1/4 teaspoon crushed red pepper flakes

1 tablespoon red wine vinegar

Kosher salt and black pepper in a mill

4 large eggs

4 4-inch polenta triangles (Polenta Shapes, page 28)

2 teaspoons minced Italian parsley

polenta buttermilk pancakes

These light pancakes have a pleasant, if subtle, taste of corn and more texture than pancakes made only with flour.

Serves 4, makes 8-10

- 1 cup boiling water
- 2 tablespoons butter
- 1 cup fine- or medium-ground polenta
- 1 tablespoon brown sugar
- 1/2 teaspoon kosher salt
- 1 1/2 cups buttermilk
- 1 cup all-purpose flour
- 1 tablespoon baking powder
- 2 eggs, beaten
- Butter

IN A MEDIUM bowl, quickly combine the water, butter, polenta, brown sugar, and salt. Stir in the buttermilk, cover, and let rest for 15 minutes. In a separate bowl, mix together the flour and baking powder, and add it to the polenta mixture, alternating with the beaten eggs.

Melt a small amount of butter in a heavy skillet or on a flat griddle. When it is hot and foamy, ladle or pour approximately 3 ounces batter for each pancake. Cook until the surface is completely covered with bubbles, turn, and cook until golden. Serve immediately, with maple syrup.

soft polenta with walnuts and gorgonzola

Although this dish can be served at any meal, it is delightful for breakfast, particularly on a cold, wintry morning. Serve with fresh fruit such as grapefruit, sliced pears, or a simple cranberry compote.

Serves 4

- 4 cups cold water
- 1 cup polenta
- 1-2 teaspoons kosher salt
- 2 tablespoons butter
- 4 ounces Parmigiano-Reggiano, Pecorino-Romano, aged Asiago, St. George, or Dry Jack, grated
- Black pepper in a mill
- 4 ounces Gorgonzola
- 2 ounces walnut halves or pieces, toasted
- Extra virgin olive oil

PLACE THE WATER in a heavy pot and stir in the polenta. Place the pot over a medium-high flame and stir the polenta constantly as it comes to a boil. Lower the heat to medium and continue stirring as the polenta thickens, about 10 minutes. Stir in the salt and butter, and continue cooking until the polenta is tender and begins to pull away from the sides of the pot. Add the grated cheese and stir until it is well incorporated. Remove the polenta from the heat, taste it, and add more salt if necessary.

At this point the polenta should be soft and creamy. If it seems a little stiff, stir in about 1/2 cup boiling water and simmer for an additional 5 minutes. Ladle the polenta into warmed soup bowls and top each serving first with a few turns of black pepper, followed by small chunks of Gorgonzola and a scattering of toasted walnuts. Serve immediately.

first courses

polenta with cheese and olive oil

Serves 4 – 6

Each November several dozen guests gather at a beautiful ranch on the edge of Dry Creek Valley in Sonoma County to pick olives from the four varieties of Italian trees—luccino, maurino, frantoio, and pendolino—that Ridgely Evers imported, the first person to do so in this century, and planted in 1990. When we return—hot, sweaty, and dusty or cold, wet, and muddy, depending on the weather—to the farmhouse with its beautiful wraparound porch, a magnificent harvest feast, prepared by Ridgely's wife, chef Colleen McGlynn, awaits us. One year, big bowls of fragrant polenta joined roasted vegetables and spit-roasted rabbit wrapped in pancetta, with plenty of luscious Fattoria Bernardini olive oil, the Italian inspiration for Ridgely's own product, to drizzle over the polenta. In this dish, one of the most basic of all polenta recipes, the quality of the ingredients, especially the olive oil, is absolutely crucial. If a genuine condiment-quality oil is not available, omit it entirely. A few hours after our feast and well before the next sunrise, the olives we picked will have been crushed and transformed into Da Vero Extra Virgin Olive Oil, a condiment oil of the first order.

Soft Polenta (page 22)

4 ounces Italian Fontina, freshly grated or sliced

Kosher salt and black pepper in a mill

Extra virgin olive oil

COOK THE POLENTA. Just before removing it from the stove, stir in the cheese. Ladle the hot polenta into large bowls, season each portion with a bit of kosher salt and several turns of black pepper, and then drizzle a tablespoon or two of olive oil over the top. Serve immediately.

Variations: Use the finest Parmigiano-Reggiano you can find and top the polenta with white truffle oil.

Any of the toppings for Polenta Crostini (page 34) (except for soppressata, prosciutto, white bean puree, and pistada) make excellent toppings for this polenta.

polenta taragna

Certain manufacturers offer something called polenta taragna in their lineup of products. The name also refers to a traditional Italian preparation that includes both cornmeal and buckwheat. The Bergamask version calls for a substantially greater quantity of butter than I have used here and a regional cheese known as formaggio di monte grassi, *or* montasio. *If you cannot locate this cheese, a domestic teleme or fresh Italian Asiago are suitable and delicious substitutes.*

Serves 4 – 6

6 cups water

1 tablespoon kosher salt

1 cup coarse-ground polenta

2 tablespoons buckwheat flour

4 tablespoons butter

2 teaspoons minced sage

6 ounces fresh Italian Asiago, sliced

Sage leaves

IN A HEAVY pot, bring 4 cups water to a rolling boil. Combine the salt, polenta, and buckwheat flour, stir the water rapidly with a whisk and, stirring in the same circular direction to create a vortex, pour the polenta mixture in a steady, thin stream, stirring vigorously all the while to prevent the formation of lumps. When the mixture returns to a boil, lower the heat so that it simmers slowly rather than boils. When the polenta begins to thicken, change from a whisk to a long-handled wooden spoon and continue to stir. Should lumps occur, use the back of the spoon to press them against the sides of the pot until they break up.

Continue to stir the polenta, being sure to reach down to the bottom of the pot, until it is thick and pulls away from the sides of the pot. Add additional boiling water as necessary. Taste the polenta to be sure the grains are tender. It will take 15 to 60 minutes to cook.

During the last 5 minutes of cooking, stir in the butter, sage, and cheese. Remove from the heat, pour into individual dishes, garnish each portion with a small sprig of sage, and serve immediately.

polenta with salami and fresh cream

Serves 4

I cannot really offer a justification for including this recipe except for the fact that when I ate it in Italy I loved everything about it: its sensational taste, of course—the cream and the salami are unlike any on this side of the Atlantic—but more than that, I admire its brazen, defiant spirit. Don't even mention fat, this recipe cries out, daring nutritionists and others to begin their lecture. While I don't recommend that you eat this often, it is one of those utterly compelling, guilty pleasures that would be a sin not to indulge in.

1 pound fresh Italian salami (salami before it has been dried)

2 tablespoons butter

1 cup heavy cream

Soft Polenta (page 22), allowed to sit long enough so that it holds its shape but is not hard

CUT THE SALAMI into slices about ⅛ inch thick. Melt the butter in a sauté pan and sauté the salami for about 2 minutes on each side. Add the cream, swirl the pan, and heat through but do not allow to boil. Remove from the heat.

Place 2 scoops of polenta on each of 4 serving plates and then divide the salami and cream among the servings. Serve immediately.

polenta with arugula sauce

Serves 4–6

I no longer recall where I first came across this combination of flavors, but the memory of that first taste lingers. I love the pleasant bitterness of arugula and find it an enticing combination with polenta.

Soft Polenta (page 22)

4 garlic cloves, minced

1 teaspoon kosher salt

3 cups arugula leaves, cleaned and trimmed

1 cup heavy cream, hot

2 ounces Parmigiano-Reggiano, grated

Black pepper in a mill

COOK THE POLENTA and when it is nearly ready, place the garlic, salt, and 2½ cups arugula in a food processor or blender and pulse until it is evenly chopped. Add half the cream and process until it is well blended. Add the remaining cream, pulse just enough to mix, transfer the sauce to a small warm bowl, and stir in the grated cheese. Keep the sauce warm.

Pour the polenta onto individual serving plates—low soup plates are ideal—and spoon the sauce over each portion. Quickly slice the reserved arugula into thin strips and scatter over the surface. Add several turns of black pepper and serve immediately.

polenta soufflé with chèvre cream

While pursuing the history of polenta in southern France and northern Italy, I had occasion to visit cooking teacher and writer Lydie Marshall, whose book Chez Nous *had just been published, in her twelfth-century chateau in Nyons in the upper reaches of Provence. I was charmed by her and her home and found the book inspiring in its direct approach to simple, good flavors. My recipe is adapted from hers.*

Serves 4 – 6

2 teaspoons butter, softened

1^1/$_2$ cups water

1 cup half-and-half

^{2}/$_3$ cup fine-ground polenta

1 teaspoon kosher salt

Black pepper in a mill

3 eggs, separated

^{1}/$_2$ cup heavy cream or half-and-half

3 ounces fresh chèvre

1 tablespoon snipped chives

BUTTER A 6 TO 8-cup soufflé dish and preheat the oven to 350°F.

In a heavy pan, combine the water and half-and-half and bring to a boil. Whisk in the polenta, stirring constantly, and cook until the polenta is the consistency of very thick cream, about 5 to 10 minutes depending on the age and type of cornmeal. Season with salt and several turns of black pepper, and remove from the heat.

Mix the egg yolks into the polenta one at a time. In an electric mixer, beat the egg whites until they form soft peaks. Using a rubber spatula, gently fold half the beaten egg whites into the polenta and when they are well incorporated, fold in the remaining egg whites. Pour the batter into the buttered soufflé dish, place in the oven, and bake for 30 minutes until the soufflé is lightly browned.

While the soufflé bakes, make the chèvre cream. With a fork, mix together the cream and chèvre until smooth. Mix in the chives, place in a small serving dish, and set aside until ready to use.

Remove the soufflé from the oven, place a spoonful of chèvre cream in the center, and serve immediately, with the remaining chèvre cream on the side.

summer tomatoes with polenta stars, chèvre, and balsamic vinegar

Serves 4

3 large or 4 medium best-quality tomatoes, sliced

1 teaspoon minced garlic

3 ounces fresh chèvre, crumbled

10–12 2-inch polenta stars (Polenta Shapes, page 28), broiled or grilled

1–2 tablespoons balsamic vinegar

4–6 tablespoons extra virgin olive oil

Kosher salt and black pepper in a mill

From the end of October until late June or July, I long for a perfect ripe tomato. My anticipation grows until they finally come into season, when I eat them daily, prepared in every way imaginable. As the season moves on, I become more and more inventive as I take advantage of their abundance. Do not make this dish unless you have top-quality tomatoes at hand.

ARRANGE THE TOMATOES on a serving plate, sprinkle the garlic over them, and then scatter the crumbled chèvre over the tomatoes. Set the polenta stars randomly over the salad. Quickly mix together the vinegar and olive oil, season it with a little salt and pepper, and drizzle it over the salad. Serve immediately.

spring greens with polenta croutons

Serves 3–4

3 tablespoons olive oil

1½ cups ¾-inch polenta cubes, cut from chilled polenta

Juice of 1 lemon

1 garlic clove, minced

¼–⅓ cup extra virgin olive oil

½ teaspoon kosher salt

Black pepper in a mill

1 quart mesclun (about 3 ounces)

2 tablespoons grated Parmigiano-Reggiano

Polenta croutons have a softer, more delicate taste and texture than croutons made of bread, and if made with high-quality polenta, they also have a rich taste of corn. Make this salad when you have leftover polenta.

HEAT THE OLIVE oil in a heavy skillet. Sauté the polenta cubes over low to medium heat, turning frequently so that each side becomes golden brown. Transfer to absorbent paper.

In a large bowl, combine the lemon juice and garlic, whisk in ¼ cup olive oil, taste, and if the mixture is too tart, add the remaining olive oil. Season with salt and pepper, add the mesclun, and with your hands quickly toss the greens in the dressing. Add the cheese, toss again, and then scatter the polenta croutons over the salad. Serve immediately.

wilted greens with grilled polenta triangles

My grandmother prepared a version of this dish for my stepgrandfather, a stern, mysterious man from Austria whom I found both intimidating and intriguing. Whenever I ate at his table, a mound of red leaf lettuce would be waiting in a white oval bowl at his side while my grandmother simmered the fragrant dressing she would pour over it. I never asked for a taste and he never offered one, and so the only signpost I had to this recipe was my memory of its evocative aroma.

Serves 4

PLACE THE LETTUCE on a large serving platter. In a small skillet, sauté the bacon until it is just crisp. Add the sugar and the vinegar; stir until the sugar is dissolved and the mixture is bubbling. Pour it over the lettuce and toss quickly. Set the grilled polenta triangles around the edge of the platter and serve immediately.

8 cups shredded lettuce (red leaf or romaine)

4 slices bacon, diced

4 teaspoons sugar

½ cup red wine vinegar

12 polenta triangles (Polenta Shapes, page 28), grilled or broiled

wilted radicchio with pancetta, chèvre, and polenta

Serves 4 – 6

Polenta and grilled radicchio are a common combination in Italy. I've added creamy fresh chèvre and a tangy dressing to create one of my favorite fall dishes, which I frequently add to my holiday table.

4 ounces bacon or pancetta, diced

1 small red onion, diced

2 pounds radicchio

¼ cup red wine vinegar

5 ounces fresh chèvre, cut into ⅓-inch slices

12 polenta triangles (Polenta Shapes, page 28), grilled or broiled

Kosher salt and black pepper in a mill

FRY THE BACON or pancetta (if using pancetta, add 2 tablespoons olive oil to the sauté pan) in a medium or large sauté pan over low to medium heat for 5 minutes. Add the onion, and sauté for an additional 10 minutes. Trim the radicchio, remove the roots, and cut each head in quarters. Place the radicchio in the pan, one of the cut sides down. Sauté for 2 minutes, and then turn the radicchio to the other cut sides. Add half the vinegar, cover the pan, and cook for 5 minutes. Transfer the radicchio to a serving platter, add the remaining vinegar to the pan, turn the heat to high, and reduce the vinegar. Arrange the grilled polenta triangles on individual serving plates, 2 per plate, and divide the radicchio among the servings, placing it on the edge of the polenta triangles so that it only covers a portion. Top each with a small round of chèvre, then divide the pan juices with the pancetta and onions among the servings, season each portion with a little salt and pepper, and serve immediately.

polenta gnocchi in broth

Polenta gnocchi have slightly more texture than gnocchi made of potatoes. They are excellent served in a light broth, but equally good tossed with one of several traditional sauces, such as ragù, pesto, or a simple cream sauce.

IN A MEDIUM saucepan, bring the milk to a boil. Add the salt and pour in the polenta in a slow, steady stream, whisking constantly. Reduce the heat to low and continue to stir the polenta until it has thickened, about 15 minutes. Remove from the heat, add the butter, stir, and let cool until the mixture is easy to handle.

In a large pot, combine the chicken broth with the herbs. Bring to a boil, and reduce the heat to a simmer.

Beat the eggs and one third of the cheese into the polenta mixture. Use a spoon to form small, oblong forms from the polenta, about the size of the first joint of an adult's thumb. Press the piece of polenta dough into the tines of a fork, rolling it along so that the fork marks the gnocchi. There should be enough dough to make approximately 72 gnocchi.

To cook the gnocchi, remove and discard the herbs from the broth and increase the heat so the broth comes to a light boil. Drop in about one third of the gnocchi, several at a time, being sure that the broth returns to a boil before adding more. Cook for 10 minutes after the gnocchi have risen to the surface. When one batch of gnocchi is done, ladle them along with some of the broth into a warm soup tureen or other container with a lid. Work quickly. When all the gnocchi have been cooked, ladle into individual soup bowls, top each portion with a sprinkling of cheese, and one or two turns of black pepper. Serve immediately.

Variation: To serve the gnocchi with sauce, remove them from their cooking liquid with a slotted spoon and place them in a warm bowl with a bit of melted butter. Toss quickly after adding each batch to the bowl so that they do not stick to each other. Suitable sauces include Pesto (page 35), Arugula Sauce (page 54), Chèvre Cream (page 55), and Ragù (page 98). Or you can serve the gnocchi simply, with butter, cheese, and minced Italian parsley.

Serves 6

2 cups milk

2 teaspoons kosher salt

7 ounces yellow polenta

1 tablespoon butter

2 quarts homemade chicken broth

1 bay leaf

1 small sprig sage

3 egg yolks, lightly beaten

3 ounces Parmigiano-Reggiano, freshly grated

Black pepper in a mill

polenta soup with swiss chard and garlic

Serves 4 – 6

6 cups water

⅓ cup polenta

4 tablespoons olive oil

3 tablespoons minced garlic (about 10 cloves)

2 bunches Swiss chard (total weight about 2 pounds), trimmed of tough stems

1 tablespoon lemon zest, minced

¼ teaspoon crushed red pepper flakes

2 teaspoons kosher salt

Black pepper in a mill

¼ cup crème fraîche (or sour cream thinned with 2 tablespoons cream)

Here, polenta provides body and structure to a soup spiked with the bright flavors of lemon and Swiss chard. Served with a salad of crispy, sliced fennel dressed with olive oil and plenty of freshly ground pepper, it makes a hearty vegetarian meal.

IN A LARGE pot, bring the water to a boil, stir in the polenta, reduce the heat to a simmer, and cook the polenta until it is tender. Meanwhile, in a large sauté pan, heat the olive oil, and sauté the garlic for 2 minutes. Slice the chard into crosswise strips about ³/₄ inch wide, add the chard to the sauté pan, and cook until limp, stirring occasionally, about 7 minutes. Add the lemon zest, toss, and add the chard to the polenta. Scrape the pan to ensure that all of the garlic makes it into the soup. Add the red pepper flakes. Continue to cook until the polenta is tender and the soup begins to thicken, 20 to 25 minutes. Taste, season with salt and pepper, ladle into soup bowls, and top each serving with a spoonful of crème fraîche.

polenta soup with sausages and sage

Serves 4 – 6

2 tablespoons olive oil

1 yellow onion, chopped

3½ cups water

2 cups chicken stock

1 pound spicy Italian sausage

2 teaspoons minced sage leaves

This version of polenta soup will please meat eaters as thoroughly as Polenta Soup with Swiss Chard and Garlic (above) pleases vegetarians.

IN A LARGE, heavy pot, heat the olive oil over medium heat, add the onion, and sauté until it is soft and fragrant, about 15 minutes. In a separate pot, combine the water and stock, and bring it to a boil. Add the sausages to the onion, brown thoroughly, stirring as necessary to keep the onion from burning, and then transfer the sausages to absorbent paper. Add the minced sage and polenta to the onion, and stir until the polenta just begins to color, 2 to 3 minutes. Add the water-stock mixture, slowly at first, whisking constantly. Add the red pepper flakes, bring the mixture to a boil, reduce the heat to a simmer, and cook until the polenta is tender, 20 to 25 minutes. While the polenta cooks, slice the cooked sausage into thin rounds, add to the pot, and stir. Stir in the cheese, season with salt and pepper, and remove from the heat. Ladle the soup into serving bowls and garnish each serving with fresh sage leaves. Serve immediately.

½ cup polenta

Pinch crushed red pepper flakes

3 ounces aged Asiago, grated

1 teaspoon kosher salt

Black pepper in a mill

Sage leaves, for garnish

onion soup with polenta croutons

Based on the classic French onion soup, this version uses a disk of polenta in place of the traditional slice of dry bread.

Serves 6 - 8

IN A LARGE, heavy pot, heat the butter and olive oil until the butter is foamy. Add the yellow onions, red onion, and leek, and sauté them over medium heat until they are very limp and fragrant, 15 to 20 minutes. Add the garlic and scallions and sauté an additional 2 minutes. Turn the heat to high, add the brandy, shake the pan, and cook rapidly until the brandy has evaporated. Lower the heat, add the wine, stock, and water, and simmer for about 20 minutes. Taste the soup, and season it with salt and several turns of black pepper.

While the soup cooks, cut the polenta into large rounds to cover the surface of the serving bowls you will use to serve the soup. Heat a bit of olive oil in a medium sauté pan and fry each polenta crouton until it is crispy and golden brown on both sides. Ladle the soup into ovenproof bowls and preheat the oven to 325°F. Carefully transfer a polenta crouton to each portion of soup, setting it carefully on top. Divide the cheese among the servings, sprinkle carefully so as not to spill the soup, set the bowls on a baking sheet in the hot oven, and bake until the cheese is fully melted and bubbly, about 10 minutes. Remove from the oven and serve immediately

3 tablespoons butter

3 tablespoons olive oil

4 yellow onions, thinly sliced

1 red onion, thinly sliced

1 leek, white part only, cleaned, peeled, and thinly sliced

1 head garlic, cloves separated and thinly sliced

1 bunch scallions, trimmed and sliced into small rounds (about ¾ cup)

¼ cup brandy

1 cup red wine

4 cups duck, veal, or beef stock

2 cups water

Kosher salt and black pepper in a mill

Firm Polenta for shapes (page 29)

Olive oil

4 ounces Fontina or Gruyère, grated

vegetarian main courses

polenta tart with summer squash salsa

Serves 4 – 6

Many people consider polenta to be winter fare, yet it lends itself to easy pairing with summer produce as well. Here, a light and tangy salsa tucked between layers of polenta makes a remarkably pleasant and refreshing summer dish. For an additional note of flavor, use Lemon Zest Polenta (page 26) or Chile and Cilantro Polenta (page 27) in place of Soft Polenta.

Olive oil

Soft Polenta (page 22)

3 green zucchini, trimmed and cut into ¼-inch dice

3 yellow squash, trimmed and cut into ¼-inch dice

1 small red onion, diced

3–4 garlic cloves, minced

1 serrano or jalapeño pepper, stemmed, seeded, and diced (optional)

Juice of 1 lime

¼ cup extra virgin olive oil

2 tablespoons butter

2 tablespoons minced cilantro leaves

Kosher salt and black pepper in a mill

3 ounces Fontina, Gruyère, St. George, Doux de Montagne, grated

BRUSH A 10-INCH tart pan or glass baking dish with a thin coating of olive oil. Prepare the polenta and while it cooks, prepare the summer squash salsa. In a medium bowl, combine the zucchini, yellow squash, onion, garlic, pepper (if using), lime juice, and olive oil. Add the cilantro leaves, and season to taste with salt and black pepper. Set aside.

When the polenta is nearly tender, stir in the butter and cheese. Pour half the polenta into the tart pan or baking dish, spoon half the salsa over, pour the remaining polenta over the salsa, and add the remaining salsa. Let rest for at least 30 minutes before serving. This dish can be refrigerated overnight and reheated in the oven.

To serve, cut the polenta tart into wedges or, if using the baking dish, cut into squares and transfer to individual serving plates.

summer polenta with fresh corn, black beans, red pepper butter, and corn salsa

Here's another highly flexible dish you can make as simple or as elaborate as time and inclination allow. The complete recipe with both sauces will add a spectacular dimension to any summer feast; omit one or both sauces and this still makes an excellent accompaniment to a summer barbecue or a delicious main course. If you are pressed for time, cook the polenta with water rather than corn stock.

WITH A SHARP knife, cut the kernels from the corn cobs, place them in a small bowl, and set them aside. Place the cobs in a large soup pot, cover with 6 cups water, bring to a boil, reduce the heat, and simmer for 15 to 20 minutes.

While the corn stock simmers, make the red pepper butter. Cut half the butter into small pieces and place in a food processor fitted with a metal blade. Add one third of the roasted red peppers, 1 tablespoon cilantro leaves, half of the serrano pepper, and the sugar, and pulse briefly. Stop the processor, use a rubber spatula to scrape the sides of the container, season the butter with salt and pepper, and pulse again until smooth. Transfer the red pepper butter to a small glass container and set it aside.

Strain the corn stock, discard the cobs, return the stock to the pot, and bring it to a boil. Add salt and then add the polenta in a slow, steady stream, stirring all the while. Bring the remaining water to a boil, reduce the heat, and simmer the polenta, continuing to stir the polenta occasionally as it cooks. Add more boiling water as necessary for the proper texture. Meanwhile, heat 3 tablespoons butter in a medium skillet. Add the remaining serrano pepper and sauté until soft, about 5 minutes. Add 1 cup corn kernels, stir, and sauté for 3 minutes. Toss with the black beans, remaining roasted red peppers, and remaining cilantro. Set aside.

When the polenta is ready, remove it from the heat and fold in the corn and bean mixture. Season with pepper and salt to taste, and stir thoroughly to

3 ears very fresh summer corn, shucked

8 cups water

4 ounces (1 stick) butter

3 sweet red peppers, roasted, peeled, seeded, and diced

3 tablespoons cilantro leaves

2 serrano peppers, stemmed and minced

1 teaspoon sugar

Freshly ground black pepper

Kosher salt

2 cups polenta

1 cup cooked black beans, drained

Corn Salsa (page 83; see Note)

Olive oil

incorporate all ingredients evenly. Place the polenta mixture into a loaf pan that has been brushed with olive oil and allow it to set up for at least 1 hour or overnight.

You can serve the polenta sliced or whole. First, unmold the polenta loaf onto a work surface or baking sheet. To heat whole, place in a preheated 375°F oven for 15 to 20 minutes until the polenta is heated through. Remove from the oven, transfer to a serving plate, top with some of the roasted pepper butter, and spoon corn salsa around the edges of the loaf.

Alternately, unmold the polenta onto a work surface, slice it into $1/2$-inch pieces, brush each piece with a bit of the roasted pepper butter, place on an oiled baking sheet, and broil until the polenta just begins to color. Transfer to individual serving plates, top with a small dollop of red pepper butter, and serve with a generous spoonful of corn salsa on the side.

N o t e : Use the corn from this recipe to make the corn salsa, reserving 1 cup for the polenta.

tomato and polenta tart with basil mayonnaise

I could eat this tart every day during tomato season. It is wonderful fresh from the oven with a green salad alongside. It is equally delicious the next day, cold, right out of the refrigerator. It also reheats quite well.

PLACE THE WATER in a heavy saucepan and stir in the polenta. Set over medium heat and bring to a boil, stirring constantly. Reduce the heat and simmer the polenta for about 15 minutes, stirring constantly until it thickens and then stirring frequently. Add the butter and stir the polenta until the butter is melted. Add the salt and flour, and stir continuously until the mixture is very thick and pulls away from the sides of the pan, 4 to 5 minutes. Remove from the heat and pour into a 10- or 12-inch tart pan that has been coated with a bit of olive oil. Using a rubber spatula, press the polenta to the bottom and sides of the pan so that it forms a crust. The polenta will be softer than chilled pie dough, but it will hold its shape. Set the shell aside until it sets up firmly, about 20 minutes.

Cut the stem ends off the tomatoes, and slice them into ¼-inch rounds. Cover the surface of the polenta shell with several whole basil leaves and arrange the tomatoes on top, making 2 layers and topping each layer with a few turns of black pepper, a bit of salt, and half the cheese. Bake in a 325°F degree oven for about 20 minutes until it is hot, slightly bubbly, and the top is just turning golden.

Meanwhile, place the remaining basil leaves and lemon juice in a blender, and pulse until the basil is pureed. Add the mayonnaise, pulse very quickly to blend well, transfer to a serving bowl, taste, and season with salt and pepper.

Remove the tart from the oven, let rest for 15 minutes, drizzle basil mayonnaise over the surface, cut into wedges, and serve, with more basil mayonnaise on the side.

2½ cups water

⅓ cup polenta

2 tablespoons butter

2 teaspoons kosher salt

¼ cup all-purpose flour

4 ripe medium tomatoes, peeled

1 cup basil leaves, loosely packed

Black pepper in a mill

4 ounces Cheddar, jack, or other mild to medium-sharp, semi-soft cheese, grated

Juice of ½ lemon

¾ cup homemade or commercial mayonnaise

polenta with tomato, onion, and artichoke sauce

Serves 6

As a California native, I take artichokes for granted, eating them with abandon during the spring, when they are inexpensive and widely available. In other parts of the country where fresh artichokes are more difficult to come by, frozen and canned ones are readily available. Although they lack the rich, nutty flavor of fresh artichokes, they are an acceptable substitute in this recipe.

4 medium artichokes, trimmed

2 tablespoons unsalted butter

4 tablespoons extra virgin olive oil

2 cups ($\frac{1}{2}$ pound) chopped yellow onions

2 teaspoons minced garlic

3 anchovy fillets, diced

1 cup dry white wine

1 14-ounce can diced tomatoes

1 teaspoon kosher salt

1 teaspoon freshly ground black pepper

Soft Polenta (page 22)

3 ounces Parmigiano-Reggiano, grated

COOK THE artichokes in a large pot of boiling water until they are tender when the bottom of the artichoke is pierced with a fork, 15 to 25 minutes, depending on the size and age of the artichokes. Drain and set them aside to cool.

Heat the butter and olive oil together in a medium skillet until the butter is melted. Add the onions and sauté over low heat until they are tender and fragrant, about 20 minutes. Add the garlic and anchovies, and sauté for another 2 minutes. Add the wine, increase the heat to high, and simmer until the wine is reduced by half, about 5 minutes. Stir in the tomatoes, reduce the heat, and simmer for 5 minutes. Add the salt and pepper, remove from the heat, and set aside.

Prepare the polenta and while it is cooking, finish the sauce. First, pull the leaves off the artichokes. Remove the choke from each heart by cutting it out with a paring knife. Trim the bottom of each heart to remove any bruised or mushy parts. Cut each heart in half lengthwise and then slice each half into $\frac{1}{8}$-inch strips. Cut off the tender, meaty tips of each leaf, making two cuts to remove the meat in thin strips. The 4 artichokes should yield 2 to 3 cups of meat. Stir it into the onion and tomato sauce, return the sauce to the stove, and heat through.

Divide the polenta among warmed serving bowls or plates, top each portion with a generous amount of sauce, and garnish with a bit of the grated cheese. Serve immediately.

ratatouille with herbed polenta

This ratatouille combines two techniques to create a rich and evocative
version of the famous vegetable stew of the south of France. Some vegetables
are roasted together so that their flavors mingle from the start; others are
cooked separately so that they retain their unique flavor and don't
overpower the other ingredients. When they are all cooked properly, they
are mixed together and allowed to rest for an hour to allow their juices
to mingle and enrich each other but not to an overwhelming degree.
The herbs in the polenta resonate with those of the ratatouille.
For a heartier dish, add grilled sausages (see Variation).

Serves 6–8

TOSS THE GARLIC cloves, mushrooms, eggplant, and onions together
and place them in a heavy roasting pan. Pour 1 1/4 cup olive oil over the vegetables, add the sprigs of thyme and oregano, and cover the pan with aluminum
foil. Bake at 350°F for 1 hour.

While the vegetables roast, peel the tomatoes by holding each over a flame
and quickly blistering the skin, letting it cool, and removing the charred skin.
Cut the tomatoes in half and gently squeeze out seeds and excess moisture. In
another roasting pan, add a little olive oil and then set the tomatoes in a flat
layer, cut side down. Roast in the oven with the other vegetables until the
tomatoes begin to darken and caramelize, 40 to 60 minutes.

Heat a small amount of the remaining olive oil in a heavy skillet and sauté
the sweet peppers until they are limp and fragrant. Transfer them to another
container and sauté the zucchini until it just begins to turn golden brown.
Add the zucchini to the peppers.

After 1 hour, test the garlic and other vegetables to be sure they are tender.
If not, cover again and let roast an additional 15 minutes. Remove from the
oven, discard the sprigs of herbs, and let the vegetables cool slightly. Check
the tomatoes and remove them from the oven when they are done. Set a large
colander over a bowl and transfer the vegetables to the colander. Let them sit
for about 10 minutes so that any excess olive oil will drain out. Break up the

8 ounces garlic cloves

**8 ounces small, whole
crimini or standard
white mushrooms**

**2 medium eggplant,
peeled and cut into 1-
inch cubes**

**3 medium yellow
onions, cut into quar-
ters**

1 3/4 cups olive oil

2 sprigs thyme

1 sprig oregano

**2 pounds ripe, red
tomatoes**

**3 sweet red peppers,
cut into medium juli-
enne**

**4 zucchini, cut into
medium julienne**

**2 tablespoons finely
minced Italian parsley**

1 tablespoon finely minced basil

1 teaspoon finely minced thyme leaves

Fresh Herb Polenta (page 26)

Kosher salt and black pepper in a mill

Small sprigs Italian parsley, basil, and thyme, for garnish

roasted tomatoes with a fork and add them to the peppers and zucchini. Gently toss together all the vegetables and the fresh minced herbs. Let the vegetables rest together for at least 1 hour so that their flavors can mingle.

While the vegetables rest, make the herb polenta. When it is done, pour it onto a large platter. Taste the ratatouille, season with salt and pepper, and spoon it onto the platter with the polenta. Alternately, allow the polenta to set up in a circle mold with an open center. Invert the polenta onto a large serving platter, spoon some of the ratatouille into the center of the mold, and spoon the rest around the outside. Garnish with sprigs of fresh herbs. Serve immediately.

Variation: Grill or broil 2 pounds of sausage and serve alongside the ratatouille and polenta. Alternately, slice the cooked sausages into rounds and fold them into the ratatouille before serving.

braised artichokes
with onions
and polenta

Prepare this recipe only when fresh artichokes are available; frozen or canned artichokes will not work here. When preparing fresh artichokes, do not use a carbon-steel knife, as it will blacken the surface of the artichoke as it cuts. Also, once exposed to air, the interior of an artichoke will turn black, so either rub any cut surface with a little olive oil or lemon juice or place cut artichokes into a bowl of water to which you have added a healthy squeeze of fresh lemon juice.

PLACE THE POLENTA in a 2-quart baking dish, add the water, salt, and butter, stir, and place in a 325°F oven for 40 minutes, open the oven door, give the polenta a quick stir, and cook for an additional 10 minutes. Remove from the oven.

While the polenta cooks, prepare the artichokes. First, trim away any tough outer leaves and cut the stems to no more than 1 inch. Using scissors, snip off any sharp tips on the remaining leaves. Cut each large artichoke into 6 lengthwise pieces (cut medium artichokes into quarters) and then remove the choke in the center of each section, using a small paring knife to cut it from the heart. Immediately place the artichokes in a large bowl of cold water and add half the lemon juice.

In a frying pan large enough to hold all the artichokes in a single layer, heat the olive oil over medium heat. Sauté the garlic cloves and onions for 5 minutes, stirring regularly; do not let the garlic burn. Using a slotted spoon, remove the garlic and onions from the pan and set them aside. Drain the artichokes, pat them dry, add them to the pan, sauté for 3 minutes, turn, and sauté for another 3 minutes. Return the onions and garlic to the pan, add the white wine and the remaining lemon juice, cover tightly, and simmer over low heat until the hearts of the artichokes are tender when pierced with a fork, 25

1 cup polenta

4 cups water

2 teaspoons kosher salt

1 tablespoon butter, cut into small pieces

3 large or 4 medium artichokes

¼ cup fresh lemon juice

¼ cup olive oil

8 garlic cloves

1 cup pearl onions, peeled (optional)

½ cup dry white wine

to 30 minutes. Remove the lid, increase the heat to medium high, and reduce the cooking liquid by half. Remove from the heat.

To serve, simply place the artichokes, onions, and garlic along with all of the pan juices on a platter and serve the polenta alongside. Alternately, you can spoon the artichokes and onions directly onto the polenta.

polenta nera with pumpkin and chard

Serves 4 – 6

This dish, rich with the dark, evocative flavors of fall and winter, makes a delicious addition to any holiday table and is equally good served on its own.

IN A SMALL bowl, mix together the polenta and buckwheat flour. Moisten with 1 cup water. Bring the remaining 3 cups water and the salt to a boil in a medium saucepan. When the water is boiling, whisk in the moistened polenta mixture, lower the heat, and stir until it begins to simmer. Simmer slowly over low heat for 20 minutes until the polenta is thick. Stir in the butter, pumpkin, nutmeg, cayenne pepper, and black pepper. Remove from the heat, stir in the cheese, and pour into a 9-inch square baking dish or tart pan coated with olive oil and let set up for 20 minutes.

Just before serving, sauté the chard in the olive oil until limp. Pass the garlic through a garlic press, add to the chard along with the lemon juice, and toss quickly. Cut the polenta into large squares, top each square with a portion of chard, set on individual plates, and serve.

½ cup polenta

2 tablespoons buck-wheat flour

4 cups water

1 teaspoon kosher salt

1 tablespoon butter

1 cup cooked pumpkin or any other winter squash, mashed

Scant ¼ teaspoon ground nutmeg

Pinch cayenne pepper

1 teaspoon freshly ground black pepper

2 ounces Asiago, grated

1 bunch (about 1¼ pound) Swiss chard or spinach, trimmed

1 tablespoon olive oil

1 garlic clove

Juice of 1 lemon

polenta loaf with mushrooms with chèvre sauce

This is a hearty and flexible dish. If wild mushrooms are available, use them; otherwise, use the most flavorful commercial mushrooms you can find. I frequently add stock to the mushrooms for an additional layer of flavor, but you can omit it and still have a delightful dish. Likewise, I use the chèvre sauce because I love the combination of flavors and textures, but it can be omitted if you prefer. This polenta loaf can be made up to 2 days in advance, covered tightly with plastic wrap, and kept refrigerated.

Serves 4 – 6

PREPARE THE POLENTA and while it cooks, prepare the mushrooms. Soak the porcinis in the hot water for at least 20 minutes. Clean the fresh mushrooms, trim away any hard stems, and break or slice the large ones, leaving the smaller ones whole. The idea is to have all the mushrooms—whole and in pieces—no larger than 2 inches. Drain the mushrooms through a sieve and save the soaking liquid. Chop the porcinis into small pieces.

Heat the butter in a large sauté pan and sauté the shallots over medium heat until they are fragrant, about 10 minutes. Add all the mushrooms, the wine, and the soaking liquid to the pan, cover, and simmer until the mushrooms are wilted and tender, 15 to 25 minutes, depending on the type of mushrooms. Remove the lid, add ½ cup stock (if using), turn the heat to high, and simmer until the liquid is nearly completely reduced. Add 3 tablespoons parsley, taste, and season with salt and pepper. When the polenta is done, fold the mushrooms into the polenta and pour the mixture into a loaf pan brushed with olive oil. Use a rubber spatula to press the mixture firmly into the pan. Let set up at room temperature for at least 1 hour; overnight is better.

To make the sauce, heat the cream and the remaining stock (if using) in a small saucepan. Add the cheese and stir over low heat until it is well incorporated into the liquid. Add the remaining parsley, taste, and season with salt and pepper.

(continued)

Polenta Taragna (page 53)

½ ounce dried porcini mushrooms

½ cup hot water

2 pounds assorted mushrooms (chanterelles, cèpes, portobello, oyster, shiitake; vary the mix depending on what is available)

4 tablespoons butter

3 shallots, minced (about ¼ cup total)

½ cup red wine

¾ cup chicken, duck, veal, or beef stock (optional)

4 tablespoons minced Italian parsley

Kosher salt and black pepper in a mill

Olive oil

1 cup heavy cream

4 ounces fresh chèvre

To serve, turn the loaf pan upside down onto a work surface or baking sheet. To serve whole, heat in a 325°F oven for 20 minutes, place on a serving platter, drizzle with a small amount of sauce, and serve the remaining sauce on the side. To serve broiled, cut ½-inch slices and place them on a baking sheet brushed with olive oil. Brush the exposed surface of the polenta loaf with olive oil and broil until the slices just begin to turn golden brown. Place a small amount of sauce on individual serving plates and set the broiled polenta slices on the sauce. Garnish with a sprig of Italian parsley and serve immediately.

Variation: Rather than folding the mushrooms into the polenta, you can layer them. Pour one third of the polenta into a baking dish or loaf pan brushed with olive oil, top with half the mushrooms, spread evenly, pour half the sauce over, followed by half the remaining polenta. Add the rest of the mushrooms and the rest of the sauce, and top with the remaining polenta. Let set up for at least 2 hours (overnight is better), heat in a 325°F oven for 25 minutes, remove from the oven, cut into squares, and serve immediately, garnished with sprigs of Italian parsley.

roman-style polenta gnocchi with sage cream sauce

Roman-style gnocchi—flat disks rather than plump dumplings—are generally made with semolina flour that has been cooked in milk, allowed to set up, cut into disks, and baked. Here, cornmeal is used in place of the semolina to create a gnocchi with slightly more texture and a wonderful taste of corn. This makes an excellent first course during a fall holiday meal when turkey will follow.

Serves 4 – 6

WHEN THE POLENTA has finished cooking, pour it onto a baking sheet that has been lightly brushed with olive oil. Use a rubber spatula dipped in cool water to spread the polenta evenly over the surface; it should be about ³/₈ inch thick. Place a sheet of parchment or wax paper brushed with olive oil on top of the polenta and allow it to cool. Place the polenta in the refrigerator for at least 2 hours; it must be very firm.

Make the sauce. Place the cream, sage sprigs, and black pepper in a heavy saucepan over medium-high heat. When the cream comes to a boil, reduce the heat to medium so that it simmers but does not boil over. Cook until the cream is reduced by one third, about 10 to 12 minutes. Remove and discard the sage sprigs, add the chèvre and stir until it is melted and smoothly incorporated into the cream. Add the minced sage, taste, and season with salt if necessary. Remove from the heat and set aside. Refrigerate until ready to use.

Preheat the oven to 325°F. Remove the polenta from the refrigerator and cut disks approximately 2¹/₂ inches in diameter. Rub the inside of a baking dish with the butter and arrange the polenta gnocchi in rows, overlapping them slightly. Heat the sauce and drizzle a small amount of it over the polenta. Place in the oven until the gnocchi are hot and just turning slightly golden. Remove from the oven, spoon more sauce over the gnocchi, garnish with fresh sage leaves, and serve immediately.

Sage-Shallot Polenta (page 27)

2 cups heavy cream

3 sprigs fresh sage

2 teaspoons freshly ground black pepper

3 ounces fresh chèvre

2 teaspoons finely minced sage

Kosher salt (optional)

1 tablespoon butter

Fresh sage leaves, for garnish

main courses with fish and shellfish

polenta with sardines and sautéed celery

If you come upon fresh sardines, by all means use them in this recipe. Simply sauté them quickly in a little olive oil. The canned version will also do just beautifully. I love their delicate, silvery appearance, which, combined with the pale green celery and yellow polenta, makes this dish as pleasing to the eye as it is to the palate.

2½ cups water

½ cup polenta

2 tablespoons butter

2 teaspoons kosher salt

¼ cup all-purpose flour

3 ounces St. George or other mild to medium-sharp semisoft cheese, grated

Olive oil

3 large stalks celery, trimmed and cut into thin, diagonal strips

2 cans (3¾ ounces each) sardines, packed in water or olive oil

Juice of 1 lemon

Black pepper in a mill

PLACE THE WATER in a heavy saucepan and stir in the polenta. Set over medium heat and bring to a boil, stirring constantly. Reduce the heat and simmer the polenta for about 10 minutes, stirring constantly until it thickens and then stirring frequently. Add the butter and stir the polenta until the butter is melted. Add the salt and flour, and stir continuously until the mixture is thick and pulls away from the sides of the pan, 4 to 5 minutes. Remove from the heat, stir in all but 3 tablespoons cheese, and pour into a 10- or 12-inch tart pan that has been coated with a bit of olive oil. Using a rubber spatula, press the polenta to the bottom and sides of the pan so that it forms a sort of crust. The polenta will be softer than chilled pie dough, but it will hold its shape. Set the shell aside until it sets up firmly, 15 to 20 minutes.

Just before serving, heat a small amount of olive oil in a heavy skillet and sauté the celery until it is just tender. Transfer the celery to the polenta shell, spreading it evenly over the surface. Open the cans of sardines, drain, remove the fish carefully so that they don't break, and place them on top of the celery. Drizzle with the lemon juice, several turns of black pepper, and a light sprinkling of kosher salt. Scatter the remaining cheese over the surface and serve immediately.

white polenta loaf
with shrimp

"The best polenta I ever had," my friend Lee told me as I was writing this book, "was somewhere in Tuscany. I was walking in the countryside when I came across a group of men who asked me to join them. One of them reached into his jacket pocket and pulled out a chunk of white polenta wrapped in paper. It was full of seafood; he broke off a piece and handed it to me. I don't know what kind of fish was in it, I don't know anything else about it except it was one of the most wonderful things I've ever eaten. The wine was good, too." I've attempted to re-create the spirit of that dish, but because Lee has long since moved away, I don't know how close to the original I've come.

Serves 4–6

COOK THE POLENTA until it is very thick and tender; when it is nearly done, prepare the shellfish. Heat the butter and garlic in a medium sauté pan, and when the butter is hot and foamy, add the shrimp and cook until they are almost done, about 3 to 4 minutes. Do not overcook them. Add the juice of 1 lemon, lemon zest, Italian parsley, and a generous pinch of salt. Remove from the heat. When the polenta is ready, fold the shrimp into it and pour it into a loaf pan that has been lined with a large piece of plastic wrap at least twice the size of the pan. Fold the plastic over the polenta loaf and let rest for 30 minutes. Weight the polenta with a small cutting board, a brick, or any other weight that will fit snugly on the loaf pan. Refrigerate for at least 4 hours until the loaf is thoroughly chilled.

To serve, unmold onto a serving plate. Mix together the remaining lemon juice and mayonnaise or aïoli, cut the loaf into ³/₄-inch slices, and serve with the sauce on the side.

aïoli

PLACE THE GARLIC and salt in a medium mortar and use a pestle to crush each garlic clove. Continue crushing and pounding the garlic until it is

Soft Polenta (page 22), made with white polenta

3 tablespoons butter

2 teaspoons minced garlic

1 pound medium shrimp, peeled, deveined, and tails removed

Juice of 2 lemons

1 tablespoon lemon zest

1 tablespoon minced Italian parsley

Kosher salt

¹/₂ cup commercial mayonnaise or aïoli

Makes about 1¹/₂ cups

fish and shellfish

8–10 garlic cloves

1 teaspoon kosher salt, plus more to taste

2 egg yolks, at room temperature

1¼–1½ cups extra virgin olive oil

1 tablespoon lemon juice (optional)

Serves 4

Soft Polenta (page 22), made with white polenta

5 pounds cherrystone clams

3 tablespoons butter

1 tablespoons minced garlic

1 tablespoons minced fresh Italian parsley

1 cup dry white wine

Juice of 1 lemon

Lemon wedges

a smooth, nearly liquid paste. Add the egg yolks, one at a time, mixing well after each addition. Set the pestle aside and begin to add the oil, drop by drop, mixing with a fork or a whisk after each addition. Gradually increase the amount of oil with each addition, but never add more oil than is completely absorbed quickly. When all of the oil has been incorporated, add the lemon juice, taste, and add additional salt if necessary. Let chill at least 30 minutes before serving. Aïoli will keep in the refrigerator for about a week.

steamed clams with creamy white polenta

In the Veneto, seafood is traditionally served with white polenta, which has a slightly gelatinous quality that some dislike. Since coarse-ground white polenta is harder to find than yellow polenta, feel free to substitute yellow cornmeal or polenta in this recipe.

COOK THE POLENTA and while it cooks, rinse the clams and discard any that do not seem to be alive (occasionally, there will be a shell full of mud and sand). Shortly before the polenta is done, heat the butter in a large pot, add the garlic and parsley, sauté over medium heat for 2 minutes, and add the wine and lemon juice. Add the clams, cover the pot, and cook until the clams just open, 3 to 4 minutes maximum.

Pour the polenta into individual serving bowls. Divide the clams among the 4 servings and then spoon some of the cooking liquid over each serving. Add a lemon wedge or two to each bowl and serve immediately.

Polenta Crostini with Simple Toppings
(page 34)

Grilled Salmon, Polenta, and Corn Salsa
(page 83)

Tomato and Polenta Tart with Basil Mayonnaise (page 67)

**Cuban Polenta Pie with Pork and Chorizo
(page 105)**

Curried Polenta with Chicken-Apple Sausages
and Chutney Sauce (page 114)

Polenta Pizza with Brie and Red Grapes
(page 43)

Polenta Pound Cake with Polenta Biscotti
(pages 129, 126)

**Soft Polenta with Walnuts and Gorgonzola
(page 50)**

mexican seafood stew with soft polenta and cilantro sauce

Achiote—a paste of ground annatto seed, cumin, garlic, vinegar, and oregano—provides an added depth of flavor in this delightful stew. Vary the seafood according to what is available—you can even omit the shellfish entirely if you wish—but do make the extra effort to locate the achiote, which can be found in most Mexican and Latino food markets.

HEAT THE OLIVE oil in a large, heavy pot and sauté the leeks and peppers until they are soft and fragrant, about 15 minutes. Add the garlic and sauté for another 2 minutes. Break up the achiote with your fingers and place it in a small bowl. Add a little of the stock and stir to make a paste. Add the achiote paste and the rest of the stock to the leek mixture, and simmer for 15 minutes. Remove ¹/₂ cup stock and set it aside. Add the zucchini and tomato pulp, and simmer for an additional 10 minutes. Add salt and pepper to taste.

While the vegetables are cooking, prepare the polenta and the cilantro sauce. Place the cilantro, garlic, and lime juice in a blender, and pulse until pureed. Add the olive oil and ¹/₂ teaspoon salt, and pulse until smooth. Transfer to a small serving bowl and set aside.

Add the seafood to the stock and vegetable mixture, cover the pot, simmer for 5 minutes, and remove from the heat. Stir the reserved stock into the polenta, divide it among heated soup bowls and then ladle the stew over it, being sure that each serving receives some of each type of seafood. Top each portion with a spoonful of cilantro sauce and serve immediately with a wedge of lime on the side.

Note: To make tomato pulp, peel ripe tomatoes by sticking one tomato at a time on the tines of a fork and scorching the skin over a gas flame or hot electric burner. Set aside briefly to cool. The skins should pull off easily. Next, remove the stem end of each tomato, cut it in half, squeeze out and discard the seeds and gel, and set aside. When all tomatoes have been peeled, cored, and seeded, chop the tomatoes until a coarse pulp is formed.

Serves 4 – 6

4 tablespoons olive oil

1 cup sliced leeks, white part only

2–3 serrano peppers, seeded and diced

6 garlic cloves, minced

3 tablespoons achiote

4 cups fish fumet or chicken stock

2 medium zucchini, diced

2 cups fresh tomato pulp (see Note)

Kosher salt and black pepper in a mill

Soft Polenta (page 22)

2 bunches fresh cilantro, cleaned and large stems removed

4–6 garlic cloves

Juice of 1 lime

¹/₂ cup extra virgin olive oil

¹/₂ pound prawns, deveined

¹/₂ pound fish fillets (snapper is ideal), cut into 1-inch cubes

2 pounds fresh mussels, trimmed and scrubbed clean, or 2 pounds cherrystone clams

1 whole lime, cut into wedges

salmon with salsa verde and white polenta

You may substitute yellow polenta for white polenta in virtually any recipe, including this one. White corn has less flavor and less protein than either blue or yellow corn; when cooked, ground white corn has a slightly gelatinous texture, so make your choice according to personal preference.

2 small or 1 medium cucumber, peeled, seeded, and diced

2 teaspoons kosher salt, plus more to taste

1 small shallot, minced

1 garlic clove, minced

2 green onions, trimmed and sliced into thin rounds

1 tablespoon minced Italian parsley

2 teaspoons small capers

2 tablespoons Champagne vinegar

2 tablespoons fresh lemon juice

$\frac{1}{3}$ cup extra virgin olive oil, plus more for seasoning the dish

Black pepper in a mill

4 fresh salmon fillets, 6 to 8 ounces each

Soft Polenta (page 22) made with white polenta

FIRST, MAKE THE salsa verde. Set cucumbers in a strainer, toss them with 2 teaspoons salt, and let them drain for 30 minutes. Squeeze out excess moisture and combine them in a medium mixing bowl with the shallot, garlic, green onions, parsley, and capers. Add the vinegar, lemon juice, and olive oil, taste, season with black pepper and, if necessary, additional salt. Cover and set aside at room temperature. Season the salmon on both sides with salt, pepper, and a little olive oil. Refrigerate until 30 minutes before grilling.

Prepare the polenta and when it is nearly done, cook the salmon either over hot coals or on a stovetop grill until it is just done, 4 to 7 minutes per side, depending on the size of the salmon. Do not overcook.

When the polenta is ready, divide it among individual serving plates and set the salmon on top of it. Spoon salsa verde over each portion of salmon and polenta, and serve immediately.

grilled salmon, polenta, and corn salsa

In this dish, each of the major elements—the fresh corn, the salmon, and the polenta—is infused with the aroma of the grill. For best results, use a charcoal grill with coals that have been started without charcoal lighter fluid, which might influence these delicate flavors.

TO GRILL OVER a charcoal fire, start the coals at least 45 minutes before you wish to eat. Otherwise, heat a stovetop grill.

Make the corn salsa. Remove the husks and silk from the corn and grill it quickly, allowing it to darken slightly but not blacken. Turn the ears so the corn will cook and color evenly. Remove the corn from the grill and set it aside to cool.

Meanwhile, remove the stem end of the tomatoes, chop them coarsely, and place them in a large mixing bowl along with the onion and peppers. Cut the corn kernels from the cobs and add them to the other vegetables. Toss the mixture together quickly, add the lime juice, oil, and cilantro, and toss again. Season to taste with salt and pepper. Set the salsa aside.

Season the salmon fillets with salt and pepper and grill, turning once after about 5 minutes. Do not overcook. While the salmon is cooking, grill the polenta triangles until they begin to turn golden brown. Place a triangle on each of 6 individual plates. Set the grilled salmon alongside the polenta triangles and spoon salsa over both. Garnish with cilantro sprigs and lime wedges, and serve immediately.

Note: Spectrum Naturals, a California company, produces an excellent, inexpensive unrefined corn oil, full of the flavor and aroma of fresh corn.

Serves 6

3 ears very fresh corn

2 ripe, red tomatoes

1 small red onion, diced

2 jalapeño or serrano peppers, with seeds, minced

1 sweet red pepper, diced

Juice of 2 limes (about $1/4$ cup juice)

$1/3$ cup unrefined corn oil (see Note) or extra virgin olive oil

$1/2$ cup cilantro leaves

Kosher salt and black pepper in a mill

6 fresh salmon fillets, approximately 6 ounces each

6 large polenta triangles (Polenta Shapes, page 28)

Sprigs of cilantro and wedges of lime, for garnish

salt cod and tomatoes with polenta

S e r v e s   4 – 6

All along the northern Mediterranean, from Spain through Provence, Italy, and Greece, salt cod in various shapes and sizes appears in stores and outdoor markets, some hanging above counters looking like nothing so much as pale exotic bats. A vendor might sell only salt cod, an inconceivable thought here, so little of this hearty specialty do we consume. In this country, I find it kept out of sight in the back room of Traverso's, a delightful Italian market near my home in Sonoma County.

½-pound piece bone-less salt cod

4 tablespoons minced garlic

¼ cup extra virgin olive oil

1 28-ounce can diced tomatoes

Bouquet garni of marjo-ram, oregano, and basil

1 cup pitted California-style black olives, sliced in half length-wise

Black pepper in a mill

Soft Polenta (page 22), Olive-Herb Polenta (page 27), or Fresh Herb Polenta (page 26)

ONE OR TWO days before preparing this dish, soak the salt cod in cool water. While it soaks, keep it in the refrigerator and change the water bath every few hours. This process leaches out excess salt.

To prepare the cod, drain it a final time, place it in a skillet or saucepan, and cover it with water. Set the pan over medium heat until the water begins to boil. Immediately remove it from the heat, cover, and let sit for 15 minutes. Drain and let cool until easy to handle.

Meanwhile, sauté the garlic in the olive oil, add the tomatoes and bouquet garni, and simmer for 10 minutes. When the cod is cool enough to handle, use your fingers to break it up into small pieces. Add the cod and the olives to the tomatoes, and simmer very slowly for 20 minutes. Add black pepper to taste.

Serve the cod over any of the suggested polentas.

bay scallops with lemon and white polenta

The same caution applies here as with other recipes calling for white polenta. In this particular combination, though, the white polenta works well with the very delicate taste and texture of the scallops.

COOK THE WHITE polenta, and about 10 minutes before it is done, prepare the scallops. Rinse the scallops and pat them dry. In a small bowl or a small paper bag, combine the flour, 1 teaspoon lemon zest, salt, and white pepper. Add the scallops and shake well in order to coat the scallops with the flour mixture. Heat the butter in a medium sauté pan and sauté the garlic over low heat for 2 minutes. Increase the heat to medium, add the scallops, toss in the pan, and sauté for about 2 minutes. Add the lemon juice, toss with the scallops, and sauté for an additional 2 minutes. Add the cream, heat through, stir in half the minced dill, and remove from the heat. Just before the polenta is done, stir in the remaining lemon zest and dill. Pour the polenta onto a serving platter, spoon the scallops and their sauce onto the polenta, garnish with lemon slices and dill sprigs, and serve immediately.

Soft Polenta (page 22) made with white polenta

1 pound fresh calico or bay scallops

$1/4$ cup all-purpose flour

3 teaspoons lemon zest

$1/2$ teaspoon kosher salt

$1/2$ teaspoon ground white pepper

2 tablespoons butter

2 garlic cloves, minced

Juice of 1 lemon

1 cup heavy cream

1 teaspoon minced dill

Lemon slices and small dill sprigs, for garnish

creamed salt cod with olive polenta and roasted peppers

Serves 4 – 6

1-pound piece salt cod

4 tablespoons olive oil

1 yellow onion, diced

6 garlic cloves, minced

2 cups whole milk

2 medium russet pota-
toes, cooked and
peeled

2/3 cup heavy cream

3 tablespoons minced
Italian parsley

1 tablespoon freshly
ground black pepper

12 polenta triangles
(Polenta Shapes, page
28)

1 large or 2 small
sweet red peppers,
roasted, peeled,
seeded, and cut into
julienne

Sprigs of Italian pars-
ley

In the early spring of 1996, I visited Barcelona for the first time. At Bar Quinn, a tiny counter eatery in the Mercado de la Boquerìa, an enormous open-air market with scores of stalls, I enjoyed more than a dozen dishes, ranging from minuscule deep-fried fish to plump veal cheeks as tender as butter. One of my favorites was a grilled pimento pepper bursting with creamed salt cod. The owner recited the recipe—in Catalán, of course, and I've done my best to re-create it here.

ONE OR TWO days before preparing this dish, soak the salt cod in cool water. While it soaks, keep it in the refrigerator and change the water bath every few hours. This process leaches out excess salt.

To prepare the cod, drain it a final time, place it in a skillet or saucepan, and cover it with water. Set the pan over medium heat until the water begins to boil. Immediately remove it from the heat, cover, and let sit for 15 minutes. Drain and let cool until easy to handle. Using your fingers, shred the cod into small pieces.

In a heavy skillet, heat the olive oil and sauté the onion until it is soft and fragrant. Add the garlic, sauté for 2 minutes, add the salt cod, and continue to cook for 5 to 7 minutes until the cod just barely begins to color. Add the milk, lower the heat, and simmer very slowly for 5 minutes. Smash the potatoes with a fork, stir them into the mixture, add the cream, and heat through but do not let boil. Stir in the parsley and black pepper.

To serve, place 2 triangles of grilled polenta on individual serving plates, spoon a generous portion of salt cod over the polenta, and garnish each portion with 2 tablespoons roasted red peppers and a small sprig of Italian parsley.

main courses with poultry

pan-roasted quail with shallots, pancetta, and polenta

Serves 4

If you don't have a ready source for good quail, the butcher at your local market can usually order them for delivery within a day or two. You may also find quail at farmers' markets, where smaller producers offer outstanding farm-raised birds. Here, I've called for boned quail because many people prefer them. If you'd rather, use quail that have not been boned.

Soft Polenta (page 22) or Sage-Shallot Polenta (page 27)

8 quail, boned

Kosher salt and black pepper in a mill

4 tablespoons olive oil

1/4 pound pancetta, cubed

8 shallots, peeled

1 tablespoon minced fresh sage

1 cup white wine

Fresh sage leaves, for garnish

PREPARE THE POLENTA and while it is cooking, prepare the quail.

Rinse the quail in cool water and pat them dry with a clean tea towel. Season the central cavity with salt and pepper, and set the quail aside. In a heavy skillet large enough to hold the quail in a single layer, heat the olive oil over medium heat. Add the pancetta and sauté until almost crisp. Using a slotted spoon, transfer the pancetta to a small dish and set aside. Add the shallots and sauté over medium heat until they are slightly browned on all sides; do not let them burn. Transfer the shallots to a small bowl or plate and set aside. Increase the heat to medium, add the quail to the pan, and brown them thoroughly on both sides. Add the sage and white wine, season with salt and several turns of black pepper, reduce the heat to low, cover tightly, and simmer for 15 minutes. Add the shallots to the skillet, replace the lid, and simmer for an additional 10 minutes. Remove the lid, add the pancetta, increase the heat, and simmer until the liquid is nearly but not completely reduced.

Allow the polenta to set up for about 15 minutes—it should be soft but not firm—place it in the center of a serving plate and set the quail on top. Add the shallots, pancetta, and pan drippings, garnish with fresh sage leaves, and serve.

oven-roasted cornish game hens with sage-shallot polenta

Here, the way in which the polenta is flavored by the juices of the game hen is thoroughly wonderful. A great time to prepare these succulent birds is when you already have cooked polenta on hand.

Serves 4

PREPARE THE SAGE-SHALLOT polenta several hours in advance. When it is done, pour it onto a baking sheet rinsed in cold water and use a rubber spatula to spread it ³/₄ inch thick. Let it cool slightly and then place it in the refrigerator, covered, until it is very firm. Remove it from the refrigerator, cut it into small cubes, and place the cubes in a medium mixing bowl. Add the minced sage and the pancetta, toss lightly, and set aside.

Preheat the oven to 350°F. Rinse the game hens inside and out, dry them thoroughly with a clean tea towel, and set them on end, central cavity down, on absorbent paper or toweling so that excess moisture can drain out. Let them sit for 5 minutes. Stuff the hens one by one. Turn the hen on end, with the cavity facing you. Season the inside with salt and one or two turns of black pepper, and then fill the cavity with about 1 cup polenta mixture. When all the hens have been stuffed, loosen the breast skin by extending your finger under the skin to loosen the membrane. Insert 2 sage leaves under each side of the breast skin of each hen and then truss or tie the hens tightly with string to close the cavities. Pour a little olive oil in the palm of one hand and rub the olive oil over the surface of the hen's skin. Season each with several turns of black pepper and a little salt. Set the hens on a roasting rack, place in a baking pan, and roast for approximately 1 hour. Remove from the oven, remove the string, and serve immediately.

Sage-Shallot Polenta (page 27), or any kind of leftover polenta

2 tablespoons minced fresh sage leaves

¹/₄ pound pancetta, cut into small cubes

4 Cornish game hens, about 1 pound each

Kosher salt and black pepper in a mill

Olive oil

16 whole sage leaves, plus more for garnish

roast chicken with lemon-scented polenta and lemon-cream sauce

Serves 4 - 6

This delicately fragrant dish demands greenery at its side. I recommend spinach sautéed with plenty of garlic, braised broccoli rabe, or, in the springtime, a mound of roasted fresh asparagus.

1 free-range chicken, about 4 pounds

Kosher salt and black pepper in a mill

Sprig of rosemary

1 small lemon, peel pricked in several places with a fork

1 small lemon, thinly sliced and seeded

3 tablespoons butter

4 tablespoons lemon zest

4 tablespoons minced Italian parsley

1/4 cup lemon juice

1 cup heavy cream

Soft Polenta (page 22)

RINSE THE CHICKEN in cool, fresh water and pat it dry with a clean tea towel. Season the inside cavity of the chicken with salt and pepper, and then place the sprig of rosemary and whole lemon in the cavity. Season the outside of the chicken with salt and pepper, and then cover the skin with the sliced lemons. Roast the chicken in a 425°F oven for about 15 minutes per pound.

To make the sauce, melt the butter in a small saucepan, add 2 tablespoons lemon zest, 1 tablespoon Italian parsley, and the lemon juice. Remove from the heat and cover. In a separate pan, reduce the cream by one third and then pour it into the lemon and butter mixture, swirling the pan to blend the ingredients. Cover the pan and set it aside.

Prepare the polenta so it is done at the same time as the chicken. Remove the chicken from the oven and let it rest for about 10 minutes before carving. Just before it has finished cooking, stir the remaining 2 tablespoons lemon zest and 1 tablespoon minced parsley into the polenta. Pour the polenta onto a large serving platter and keep it warm. Carve the chicken and set the pieces in a circle around the edge of the polenta. Drizzle a bit of the sauce over both the polenta and the chicken, scatter the remaining parsley over all, and serve immediately with the remaining sauce on the side.

Variation: For a lighter (and lower fat) version of this dish, substitute chicken stock for the cream. Reduce it by half before adding it to the lemon-butter mixture.

chicken with soft polenta and broccoli rabe

This is one of those dishes that doesn't really need a recipe; it's a winning combination requiring only that you not mess with it too much.

If you want to jazz it up a bit, coat the chicken with some good Dijon mustard instead of olive oil and stir a little mustard powder mixed with cold water into the polenta. Or drizzle the final dish with about 1/4 cup of the best extra virgin olive oil you can get your hands on.

Serves 4

RUB THE CHICKEN with some olive oil and season it with salt and pepper. Squeeze the juice of a lemon over it and let it sit for an hour. Place the chicken on a baking rack in a roasting pan and roast it in a 400°F oven until cooked, 30 to 50 minutes, depending on how well done you like your chicken.

About 20 minutes or so before the chicken will be ready, place 1 cup chicken stock and the water in a heavy pot. Place the pot over medium heat, whisk in the polenta, and add the salt and butter. Stir until the polenta comes to a boil and begins to thicken. Lower the heat and stir occasionally while it cooks. Steam the broccoli rabe in the remaining chicken stock and keep it warm.

When the chicken is done, remove it from the oven and place it on a warm plate. Over low heat, deglaze the pan with the cooking liquid from the broccoli rabe. Pour the polenta in a large serving dish, arrange the chicken and the broccoli rabe on top, and pour the pan juices over it all. Serve immediately.

1 chicken, cut up (free range, if available; they taste better)

Extra virgin olive oil

Kosher salt and black pepper in a mill

1 lemon

2 cups chicken stock

3 cups cold water

1 cup polenta

1 teaspoon salt

1 tablespoon butter

2 bunches broccoli rabe

spicy chicken and garlic with creamy polenta

Serves 4

If you believe that garlic is garlic is garlic, you are in for a pleasant surprise. There are hundreds of varieties of garlic, and numerous farmers around the country specialize in growing them. One such farmer, Chester Aaron, has recorded his experiences in a lovely memoir, Garlic Is Life (Ten Speed Press, 1996). If you need inspiration, you need look no further than this charming treatise to the world's most aromatic lily. Try this recipe not with California White, the most commonly cultivated garlic clove, but with Spanish Roja, Creole Red, Asian Tempest, Inchelium Red, or any one of many different kinds of garlic available from specialty producers (see Resources, page 133).

4 firm heads garlic

2 tablespoons olive oil

2 tablespoons butter

1 4- to 5-pound free-range chicken, cut up

1 cup homemade chicken stock

1 cup dry white wine

4 jalapeño peppers

Soft Polenta (page 22)

½ cup cilantro leaves

Kosher salt and black pepper in a mill

CUT EACH HEAD of garlic in half crosswise, as you would a grapefruit (see Note). Heat the oil and butter in a large saucepan and sauté the garlic, cut side down, over medium heat until it just begins to brown. Remove from the pan and set aside. In the same pan, sauté the chicken until it is golden brown on all sides. Return the garlic to the pan, add the chicken stock, wine, and jalapeño peppers, and cover the pan with a tight-fitting lid. Braise over low heat until the liquid is reduced and thickened and the garlic cloves are very soft, about 45 minutes.

Meanwhile, prepare the polenta. To serve, arrange the garlic, peppers, and chicken on a serving platter. Pour the polenta into a large serving bowl, spoon the pan juices from the chicken over the polenta, scatter a few of the cilantro leaves over, and add salt and pepper. Scatter the remaining cilantro leaves over the chicken, garlic, and peppers, and serve immediately. To eat the garlic, use a small fork to pluck it from its sheath of skin.

Note: Depending on the type and size of the garlic, the stem half may separate into individual cloves; the root end will remain connected to the root stump. Do not fret. Just sauté the cloves as they are, connected or separate. They will be delicious either way.

chicken *au vinaigre* with polenta

The voluptuously rich sauce that brings this dish together has its roots in the Loire Valley of France, where sultry hot summers guaranteed that some of the region's wine would inevitably turn to vinegar. An industrious people, they transformed the loss into a delicious cuisine, and the town of Orléans at the northernmost point of the valley became known as the vinegar capital of the world. In spite of the seemingly large quantity of vinegar called for here, this version of the ancient dish is only mildly tart.

CUT THE CHICKEN into breast-wing and thigh-leg pieces. Rinse and dry the chicken, and rub it with salt and pepper. Melt the butter in a large, heavy frying pan over medium heat, and add the chicken, browning it until deep golden on both sides. Add the garlic and turn frequently to brown it, but do not let it burn. Sprinkle 2 tablespoons each chives and parsley over the chicken, cover the pot, lower the heat, and let the chicken simmer gently for 20 minutes.

After 20 minutes, transfer the chicken to a warm dish, cover, and place in a warm oven. Turn the heat up under the sauté pan and add the vinegar, scraping and deglazing the pan quickly. Add the stock and 2 tablespoons tomato paste. Stir constantly until the sauce reduces by half. Remove the garlic cloves. Press the pulp out of the cooked garlic with a fork, discard the skin, and blend the pulp into the sauce. Strain the sauce, return it to the pan, and set it aside.

Prepare the polenta. To complete the sauce, place the pan over low heat and stir 1/4 cup cream into the sauce. Taste the sauce and add the remaining cream if it is too tart for your palate. Do not let the sauce boil. Taste again, adjust the seasonings, and add the remaining chopped herbs. Return the chicken to the sauce, turn to coat it thoroughly, and leave it on the heat for 10 minutes, making sure it does not boil. To serve, pour the polenta onto a large serving platter, set the chicken around the edges, and spoon the sauce over all. Garnish with the sprigs of fresh herbs and serve immediately.

1 3½-pound roasting chicken

Kosher salt and black pepper in a mill

4 tablespoons butter

6 garlic cloves, unpeeled

4 tablespoons snipped chives

4 tablespoons minced Italian parsley

³/₄ cup red wine vinegar

8 ounces duck or veal stock

2 tablespoons sun-dried tomato paste or double-concentrated tomato paste

Sun-dried Tomato Polenta (page 26)

¹/₄–¹/₂ cup heavy cream

Sprigs of Italian parsley and chives

drunken chicken with olives and polenta

I have enjoyed several versions of this fragrant Mexican stew and particularly like this one, developed specifically to go with polenta.

3 tablespoons olive oil

8 chicken thighs (see Note)

2 yellow onions, cut into ¼-inch rounds

6 garlic cloves, thinly sliced

3–4 serrano or jalapeño peppers, sliced in small rounds

1 teaspoon toasted cumin seed

1½-inch stick cinnamon

½ teaspoon whole black peppercorns

6 allspice berries

¾ cup medium dry sherry

4 ounces salt-cured black olives

Kosher salt

Chile-Cilantro Polenta (page 27) or Olive-Herb Polenta (page 27)

2 tablespoons minced cilantro

PLACE THE OLIVE oil in a heavy, ovenproof skillet large enough to hold the chicken in a single layer, and set it over medium heat. Brown the chicken on both sides and transfer it to a plate. Add the onions and sauté for 10 minutes. Add the garlic and peppers, and sauté for an additional 2 minutes. Add the spices, sherry, and olives, and season with salt. Return the chicken to the skillet, cover with a tight-fitting lid, and place in a 325°F oven for 45 minutes until the chicken is very tender. Remove from the oven and serve with chile-cilantro polenta or olive-herb polenta. Garnish with the minced cilantro.

Note: I prefer both the flavor and texture of chicken thighs, and use them whenever possible. However, any part of the chicken—legs, breast, or even a whole chicken, cut into pieces—can be used in this recipe.

orange-scented duck with olives and polenta

In anticipation of the subtle orange flavor of this duck, I liked to begin the meal with an appetizer of peeled orange slices drizzled with an excellent extra virgin olive oil, seasoned with a bit of kosher salt and plenty of freshly ground black pepper, and topped with thin curls of Parmigiano-Reggiano.

RINSE THE DUCK in cool water and pat it dry with a tea towel. Prick its skin in several places, being carefully not to puncture the meat. Set the duck on a roasting rack over a shallow baking pan, place it in a preheated 425°F oven, and roast it for 30 minutes, basting every 10 minutes or so with any fat that has rendered. Remove the duck from the oven, discard the fat that has collected in the baking dish, and reduce the oven temperature to 325°F.

In a heavy ovenproof pot, combine the red wine, stock, orange zest, orange juice, ginger, cloves, cinnamon, and bouquet garni. Bring the mixture to a boil and remove from the heat. Season the duck inside and out with salt and several turns of black pepper, and place it in the pot with the wine mixture. Add the olives, cover the pot, place in the oven, and cook until the duck is very tender, about 1 to 1¼ hours. While the duck cooks, prepare the polenta and allow it to set up briefly.

Remove the duck from the oven, transfer it and the olives to a platter, and keep them warm. Remove and discard the bouquet garni from the sauce, pour the sauce into a narrow, clear container, allow the juices to settle to the bottom, and then remove the fat with a spoon and discard it. Return the sauce to the pot or a small saucepan and reduce it to about ³/₄ cup. Taste and correct the seasoning with salt and pepper, if necessary, and pour the sauce into a small serving bowl.

To serve, carve the duck, place the polenta in the center of a large serving platter, surround it with the sliced duck, and scatter the olives over all. Serve immediately, with the sauce on the side.

Serves 4

1 4- to 5-pound duck

1 cup red wine

1 cup chicken, duck, or veal stock

1 tablespoon minced orange zest

Juice of 2 oranges

2 ¹/₂-inch slices fresh ginger

4 whole cloves

1¹/₂-inch piece stick cinnamon

Bouquet garni of fresh thyme, marjoram, and Italian parsley

Kosher salt and black pepper in a mill

8 ounces salt-cured olives

Soft Polenta (page 22)

main courses
with meat

polenta with ragù

Serves 6-8

Polenta layered with a rich ragù is a classic Italian combination. The richest of the tomato-based sauces, ragù offers an unsurpassed creamy depth of flavor. Long, slow cooking mingles the flavors and textures of various ingredients to create an earthy, evocative sauce. This is Italian comfort food at its finest, and it is the sauce that made Bologna, in northeastern Italy, famous. Whenever you see alla Bolognese *on a menu, it refers to this traditional mixture of slowly cooked beef and tomatoes (though it is not always the real thing that you are served). Combined with polenta, ragù is frequently served on feast days.*

4 tablespoons butter

4 tablespoons olive oil

1 medium yellow onion, chopped

2 stalks celery, strings removed and finely chopped

1 carrot, peeled and finely chopped

2 pounds lean ground beef

1 teaspoon kosher salt

2 cups dry white wine

1 cup milk

Generous pinch nutmeg

2 28-ounce cans plum tomatoes, with juice

Soft Polenta (page 22)

3 ounces Parmigiano-Reggiano, grated

HEAT THE BUTTER and olive oil in a heavy, deep pot. Add the onion and sauté it over medium heat until it is soft and translucent, about 15 minutes. Add the celery and carrot, and cook for an additional 2 minutes. Add the beef and crumble it with a fork as it cooks. Continue to stir the meat until it loses its raw color but has not begun to brown. Add the salt and wine, turn up the heat, and simmer until the wine evaporates. Lower the heat, add the milk and nutmeg, and cook gently, stirring continuously, until the milk evaporates.

Add the tomatoes, break up the tomatoes with a fork, stir the mixture, and when it is thoroughly heated and begins to simmer, lower the heat and cook the sauce at the *barest* hint of a simmer for $3^1/2$ to 4 hours. The sauce can be made 2 to 3 days in advance and reheated. It can also be frozen.

To complete the dish, pour one third of the polenta into a large ovenproof dish and ladle the sauce over the surface. Repeat with another layer of polenta, more sauce, a final layer of polenta and the cheese. Let it set up for 20 minutes and then bake in a preheated 350°F oven for 35 minutes until the top is just slightly golden. Remove from the oven, let rest for 10 minutes, and serve.

short ribs with pancetta and herb polenta

Here, polenta takes the place of a more traditional accompaniment, mashed potatoes, though you will frequently see the two paired in Italy.

Serves 4–6

PREHEAT THE oven to 300°F. In a heavy, ovenproof skillet, sauté the diced pancetta over medium-low heat until it is brown and almost crispy. Stir frequently so that it does not burn. Transfer the pancetta to a small dish and set it aside.

Add the short ribs and brown them thoroughly on both sides (do this in two batches, if necessary, so that you have just a single layer of ribs in the skillet at one time). Transfer the short ribs to a plate and set aside.

Add the olive oil to the skillet, heat it through, add the onion and leeks, and sauté until soft and fragrant, about 15 minutes. Do not let brown. Add the garlic and sauté for 2 minutes. Add the red wine, stock, and tomato paste, and stir. Add the bouquet garni and bay leaf, and return the short ribs to the skillet. Season with 1 teaspoon salt and several turns of black pepper, scatter the pancetta over the top and cover the skillet with a tight-fitting lid. Bake for 2 hours until the short ribs are very tender and the liquid is reduced by two thirds.

Remove from the oven, let rest for 5 minutes, remove the bouquet garni and bay leaf, and serve with herb polenta.

¼ pound pancetta, diced

2½ pounds beef short ribs, cut into single rib lengths

3 tablespoons olive oil

1 yellow onion, peeled and diced

2 small leeks, white part only, cleaned and thinly sliced

6 garlic cloves, thinly sliced lengthwise

¾ cup red wine

¾ cup beef or veal stock

1 tablespoon double-concentrated tomato paste

Small bouquet garni of rosemary, thyme, and Italian oregano

1 bay leaf

1 teaspoon kosher salt

Black pepper in a mill

Fresh Herb Polenta (page 26)

italian
shepherd's pie

Traditional shepherd's pie, from the British Isles, consists of a stew of ground beef and onions smothered under a mound of creamy mashed potatoes. This recipe borrows from both Italian and British traditions to create a hearty, flavorful winter stew.

**Fresh Herb Polenta
(page 26)**

**¹/₂ ounce Italian dried
wild mushrooms**

1 cup lukewarm water

**2 tablespoons clarified
butter**

**1 pound yellow onions,
chopped**

**3 ounces pancetta,
diced**

**2 pounds lean ground
beef**

³/₄ cup red wine

6 garlic cloves, minced

**1 tablespoon minced
oregano**

**¹/₄ cup minced Italian
parsley**

**1 28-ounce can diced,
sliced, or crushed
tomatoes**

**Kosher salt and black
pepper in a mill**

BRUSH A 3-QUART baking dish lightly with olive oil. Prepare the herb polenta and while it cooks, prepare the beef mixture. First, soak the mushrooms in the lukewarm water for at least 20 minutes. In a large, heavy frying pan, heat the butter and add the onions. Sauté over low to medium heat until the onions are fragrant and translucent, about 15 minutes. Stir in the pancetta and sauté for another 5 minutes. Add the beef, crumble it with a fork, and stir until it just loses its pink color, about 8 minutes. Remove the mushrooms from their soaking liquid, chop them, and add them to the beef mixture. Strain the mushroom liquid, and add to the beef along with the wine and the garlic. Simmer until the liquid has evaporated. Stir in the oregano, parsley, and tomatoes. Simmer for 10 minutes. Add salt and pepper to taste. Transfer the beef mixture to the baking dish, distributing it evenly.

Pour the herb polenta over the top of the beef mixture and bake in a 350°F oven until the top of the polenta is just beginning to color and the mixture beneath is bubbling, about 25 minutes. Remove from the oven and let rest for 10 minutes before serving.

pork tenderloin with lavender-infused polenta and currant sauce

This polenta, served without the pork but with the currant sauce, is excellent as a side dish or, accompanied by a green salad, as a main-course lunch. Vegetarians might add slices of grilled eggplant in place of the meat. If lavender flowers are difficult to come by, you can simply omit that step and still have a great dish. The currant sauce can be made several days in advance and kept refrigerated until ready to use.

Serves 6–8 as a main course

SET THE PORK tenderloins on a work surface and remove large pieces of fat, if any (you can also remove the membranelike covering called the silver skin, using a very sharp knife). Combine 2 teaspoons lemon zest with 1 teaspoon salt and several turns of black pepper. Rub half the mixture into each pork tenderloin, set on a plate, cover, and refrigerate up to 4 hours until 30 minutes before cooking.

In a heavy saucepan, simmer the half-and-half and lavender flowers together over medium heat for 5 minutes. Remove from the heat, cover, and let steep for 30 minutes. Strain the mixture and discard the flowers. Prepare the currant sauce.

Prepare the polenta. When it is nearly done, stir in the lavender infusion and the remaining lemon zest. Add the butter and cheese, taste, and season with salt and pepper to taste. Remove the polenta from the heat and pour it onto a large serving platter.

While the polenta cooks, prepare the pork tenderloins. Set them on a roasting rack, set the rack on a baking sheet, and place in a 375°F oven for 20 minutes, or until they are just done and still slightly pink in the middle. Remove them from the oven and let rest for 5 minutes. Cut the tenderloins into 1/4-inch slices and place the slices either on top of or alongside the polenta. Drizzle a small amount of the currant sauce over the pork and polenta, garnish with lavender flowers, if using, and serve the remaining sauce on the side.

(continued)

2 pork tenderloins, about 1 to 1¼ pounds each

1 tablespoon lemon zest, finely minced

1 teaspoon kosher salt, plus more to taste

Black pepper in a mill

½ cup half-and-half or whole milk

2 tablespoons dried lavender flowers (optional)

Currant Sauce

Soft Polenta (page 22)

2 tablespoons butter

1½ ounces St. George, Fontina, or Gruyère, grated

1 cup balsamic vinegar, plus more to taste

1¹⁄₂ cups currants

1 cup dry white wine

¹⁄₄ cup dried lavender flowers

¹⁄₂ cup brown sugar, plus more to taste

Juice of 1 lemon

2 teaspoons lemon zest, finely minced

1 tablespoon butter

currant sauce

Pour the balsamic vinegar over the currants and let soak for about 1 hour. In a nonreactive saucepan, simmer the white wine and lavender flowers until the wine is reduced by half. Remove from the heat and let steep for 30 minutes. Strain the white wine into the currant and vinegar mixture and discard the lavender flowers. Place the currants and the liquid into a large saucepan, add the sugar and lemon juice, and simmer over low heat for 30 minutes. Remove from the heat and let cool.

Puree the sauce in a blender and strain it through a sieve, pressing and squeezing the pulp to extract as much liquid as possible. Discard the solids, return the strained sauce to the saucepan, stir in the lemon zest, and taste for sugar and acid. Add more sugar or more balsamic vinegar to achieve a pleasing balance. Just before serving, warm the sauce thoroughly and swirl in the butter until it is just melted.

roast pork loin with apricot sauce and polenta pilaf

In her book Savoie: The Land, People, and Food of the French Alps, *French chef and author Madeleine Kamman tells a delicious story of polenta and how it is used in Savoie, the intriguing land nestled in the mountainous terrain of eastern France near the borders of Switzerland and Italy. Corn, she tells her readers, arrived in the Savoie in the early 1700s as seeds brought from nearby Piedmont. Until 1780 it was used only to feed animals, but by the time of the French Revolution near the end of the century and the resulting shortages of foods, cornmeal had become a staple.*

Polente au bâton, so-named for the large stick used to stir it, is virtually identical to its traditional Italian counterpart. A second technique resembles that used to make pilaf. Very coarse-ground cornmeal is stirred into onions that have been sautéed in butter and only then is the boiling liquid—water, broth, or bouillon—added. The polenta is then baked in an oven and fluffed with a fork before it is served as a traditional accompaniment to snail fricassee, sausages, a cherry ragoût called Bregye, or with dried pears and prunes. This version, made with pancetta, dried apricots, and toasted pine nuts, is inspired by Madeleine's recipe.

Serves 6

MAKE THE apricot sauce. Place the pork roast on a roasting rack in a heavy pan, place in an oven preheated to 325°F, and roast for 20 to 25 minutes per pound until it reaches an internal temperature of 160°F. While the pork cooks, baste frequently with the apricot sauce.

Prepare the polenta so it will be ready when the pork is ready. Melt 2 tablespoons butter in a heavy skillet, add the onion, and sauté until soft and fragrant. Add the polenta, and stir for 2 or 3 minutes while the polenta picks up a little color. Do not let burn. Slowly pour in the stock, stirring with a whisk all the while in order to prevent lumps. Cover with a tight-fitting lid and place

1 small loin pork roast, about 2½ pounds

Apricot Sauce

3 tablespoons butter

1 yellow onion, minced

1 cup coarse-ground yellow polenta (see Note)

4 cups chicken stock or water, boiling

¼ pound pancetta, diced

¾ cup dried apricots, minced

½ cup pine nuts, lightly toasted

Kosher salt and black pepper in a mill

in the oven with the pork roast until all of the liquid has been absorbed and the polenta is tender, about 40 minutes.

In a small sauté pan, cook the pancetta until it is almost crisp, add the dried apricots and pine nuts, and set aside.

When the pork roast is done, remove it from the oven, let it rest for 10 minutes, and slice it very thinly. Remove the polenta from the oven, add the remaining butter and the pancetta mixture, and toss with a fork. Place the polenta in the center of a serving platter and surround it with slices of pork. Season with salt and several turns of pepper. Drizzle a bit of apricot sauce over all and serve immediately. Pass the remaining apricot sauce.

Note: The cornmeal I prefer for this dish is a very coarse-ground organic polenta from Gray's Gristmill (see Resources, page 133).

apricot sauce

Makes approximately 2 cups

2 tablespoons olive oil

1 yellow onion, diced

4 garlic cloves, minced

1/2 teaspoon ground cinnamon

1/2 teaspoon cumin seeds, toasted

1/2 teaspoon ground cumin

2 whole cloves, coarsely ground

Pinch of nutmeg

8 ounces apricot jam

1 1/2 cups medium-dry white wine

In a medium saucepan, heat the olive oil, add the onion, and sauté over medium heat until soft and translucent, about 15 minutes. Add the garlic and sauté an additional 2 minutes. Add the spices, stir, and add the apricot jam. Stir continuously as the jam melts, pour in the wine, stir until the sauce is smoothly blended, and simmer for 15 minutes. Remove from the heat and keep warm until ready to serve.

cuban polenta pie with pork and chorizo

Cuban cornmeal, available in Hispanic markets, is more finely ground than either Italian polenta or American cornmeal, but it is used in a similar manner: eaten as a porridge with either sweet or savory accompaniments and baked and served with meat, fish, or chicken. The classic dish known as Harina Rellena, a cornmeal pie with ground beef, tomatoes, raisins, green olives, and potatoes, serves a crowd in much the same way as polenta topped with marinara sauce might. Here, I've used several traditional Cuban recipes to inspire my version of a Cuban polenta pie.

IN A NONREACTIVE bowl, toss the pork with the juice of 1 lime, season it with salt and pepper, and marinate it in the refrigerator for a minimum of 2 hours and up to 4 hours. Remove the pork from the refrigerator and drain and discard the marinade. Heat 2 tablespoons olive oil in a heavy skillet, add the onion, and cook over medium heat until it is tender and fragrant, about 15 minutes. Add the green pepper and sauté until it is limp, about 10 minutes. Add the garlic and sauté for 2 minutes. In a separate sauté pan, cook the pork in about 1 tablespoon hot olive oil until it is browned on all sides. Add the pork to the onion mixture. Sauté the chorizo separately, using a fork to break it up, and when it is nearly done, drain off the excess fat, and add it to the pork and onion. Increase the heat to high, add the sherry and the remaining lime juice, and cook until the liquid is reduced by two thirds. Stir in the tomatoes, cumin, and Tabasco sauce, reduce the heat to low, cover the pot, and simmer the mixture for 20 minutes. Taste the stew and season with salt and pepper as necessary.

Meanwhile, cook the polenta. When it is tender, pour half of it into a large ovenproof baking dish. Spread the pork mixture over the polenta, scatter the olives over the pork, and pour the remaining polenta over all. Bake in a 350°F oven for 35 minutes until the polenta begins to turn golden on top. Remove from the oven and let sit for 10 minutes before serving with the cilantro leaves scattered over the top.

Serves 6-8

1 pound pork shoulder, cut into ¹/₂-inch cubes

Juice of 2 limes

Kosher salt and black pepper in a mill

3 tablespoons olive oil

1 medium yellow onion, chopped

¹/₂ green bell pepper, chopped

6 garlic cloves, minced

¹/₂ pound chorizo sausage

¹/₂ cup dry sherry

2 cups peeled, seeded, and chopped Roma tomatoes or, if not in season, 2 cups canned crushed tomatoes

1 teaspoon ground cumin

1 teaspoon Tabasco sauce

Soft Polenta (page 22) or Chile-Cilantro Polenta (page 27)

1 cup green olives, pitted and sliced in half

2 tablespoons minced cilantro leaves

soft polenta with lamb shanks, chard, and garlic

Serves 4

Recently, numerous restaurant chefs have discovered lamb shanks. They are enormously popular and quite inexpensive, something home cooks have known for a long time. Lamb shanks should always be cooked long and slow, so that the meat almost falls off the bone and is fork tender. Served with a fragrant polenta and tangy chard redolent with garlic, this dish makes an outstanding meal in cold weather.

4 lamb shanks, about $^3/_4$ pound each

Olive oil

10 garlic cloves, unpeeled

2 leeks, white and pale green parts only, cleaned and cut into $^1/_2$-inch rounds

2 cups red wine

3 cups veal or beef stock

Bouquet garni of Italian parsley, oregano, marjoram, thyme, summer savory, and rosemary

Soft Polenta, oven method (page 24)

2 bunches (about 2 pounds) Swiss chard, washed, dried, and trimmed

2 tablespoons lemon zest

Kosher salt and black pepper in a mill

PREHEAT THE OVEN to 350°F. Trim the lamb shanks, removing the fell (thin, outer paperlike membrane) and any accessible fat. Heat the olive oil in a deep, heavy skillet and sauté 7 garlic cloves in their skins until they just start to color. Do not let them brown. Remove the garlic cloves and set them aside. Add the shanks to the skillet and brown them thoroughly on all sides, about 10 minutes in all. Remove the shanks, drain off all but 2 tablespoons fat, sauté the leeks for about 7 minutes until they are just wilted, and return the garlic and the shanks to the skillet. Add the red wine, stock, and bouquet garni. Cover the skillet, place it in the oven, and cook for $1^1/_2$ hours. Remove the lid and cook for an additional 30 minutes.

Begin cooking the polenta when you remove the lid from the lamb. Remove the shanks from the oven, transfer them to a platter, and keep them warm. Skim off any fat from the cooking liquid, discard it, and transfer all but $^1/_4$ cup of the cooking liquid to a serving bowl. Peel and mince the remaining garlic and add it to the skillet. Place the chard in the skillet, place the skillet over medium heat, cover, and cook until the chard is complete wilted, about 8 minutes. Remove the lid, add 1 tablespoon lemon zest, and toss the chard with the juices and the zest. Remove the polenta from the oven, taste it, add salt, several turns of black pepper, and the remaining lemon zest. Pour the polenta onto a large serving platter. Spoon some of the shank cooking liquid over the polenta and then top the polenta with the chard and its juices. Either arrange the shanks around the edge of the platter of polenta, or serve them on a separate platter. Serve immediately with the cooking liquid on the side.

polenta loaf with lamb, spinach, olives, and feta

Here, rich lamb and the tangy flavors of feta cheese, olives, lemon, and tomato join aromatic rosemary and oregano in a savory Greek pie. Serve with a salad of sliced tomatoes, onions, red peppers, and cucumbers dressed with olive oil and red wine vinegar, which will provide a bright, sparkling contrast to the richness of the pie itself.

Serves 6

COOK THE POLENTA and while it cooks, prepare the lamb. First, heat the olive oil in a medium skillet. Sauté the garlic over low heat for 2 minutes, increase the heat to medium, add the spinach, cover the skillet, and cook until the spinach is wilted, 2 to 3 minutes. In a separate skillet, cook the lamb over medium heat until it loses its pink color, breaking it up with a fork while it cooks. Drain and discard excess fat, and add the lamb to the spinach. Add the olives, the feta, rosemary, oregano, pepper, and salt to taste, toss together, and set aside until the polenta is ready.

Meanwhile, prepare the sauce. Combine the tomato sauce and stock in a small saucepan, and bring to a boil. Reduce the heat to a simmer, add the lemon juice, lemon zest, oregano, cinnamon, black pepper, and salt, and simmer for 5 minutes. Remove from the heat and set aside.

Brush the inside of a loaf pan with a thin coating of olive oil. When the polenta is done, pour half of it into the loaf pan, place the lamb mixture over the surface, and top with the remaining polenta. Let the loaf set up for at least 30 minutes. Bake in a 325°F oven for 30 minutes, remove from the oven, and let rest for 10 minutes. Heat the sauce, remove and discard the cinnamon, and serve the polenta with the sauce on the side.

Soft Polenta (page 22)

2 tablespoons olive oil

8 garlic cloves, minced

1 bunch spinach, rinsed and sliced

2 pounds ground lamb

1 teaspoon finely minced rosemary

1 teaspoon finely minced Greek oregano

1 cup Kalamata olives, pitted and sliced lengthwise

6 ounces feta, cut into 1/2-inch cubes

1 teaspoon freshly ground black pepper

Kosher salt

Olive oil

Sauce
3/4 cup tomato sauce

1/2 cup chicken or beef stock

Juice of 1 lemon

1 teaspoon minced lemon zest

1 teaspoon oregano

1-inch piece stick cinnamon

2 teaspoons freshly ground black pepper

1 teaspoon kosher salt

main courses
with sausage

polenta with sausage, summer onions, and sweet peppers with Romesco sauce

Serve 4 – 6

Soft Polenta (page 22)

12 small red onions

Olive oil

6 sweet red peppers

12 hot Italian sausages

Romesco Sauce

Young onions are tender and sweet, perfect for grilling and eating just as they are, accompanied by a flavorful sauce. Here, they are paired with a traditional Catalán condiment, Romesco Sauce, served in Spain with a variety of dishes, including the exquisite, delicate spring onion calçot.

PREPARE THE POLENTA and when it is done, place it in a decorative mold and set it aside. While the polenta cooks, prepare the onions. First, remove the outer papery skins and trim off any excess root. Preheat the oven to 375°F or prepare an outdoor grill. Rub the onions with a small amount of olive oil, place them on a rack over a baking pan, and bake in the oven until they are very tender, 30 to 40 minutes. (Alternately, leave their papery skins intact and grill them over medium-hot coals, far enough from the fire that they cook before they become completely charred.) Cut the peppers in half, remove the stems and seed cores, and place them, cut side down, on a baking sheet. Drizzle a small amount of olive oil over the peppers, place them in the oven, and bake them until the skins begin to char and separate from the flesh (the peppers, too, may be prepared on the grill). Remove them from the oven, let cool slightly, and peel off the skins. Broil or grill the sausages until done.

To serve, unmold the polenta into the center of a large platter and surround it with the onions, peppers, and sausages. Serve with Romesco Sauce on the side.

romesco sauce

2 small dried red chile peppers

2 egg yolks, at room temperature

¼ cup toasted, slivered almonds

Two hours before making the sauce, cover the dried chile peppers with hot water and set them aside. Drain the dried peppers and place them in a food processor along with the egg yolks, garlic, and almonds, and process until a smooth paste forms. Add the sweet pepper and tomato, and process until smooth. With the machine running, slowly add half the olive oil. Stop the processor as necessary to push ingredients down from the sides of the container. Continuing to process, slowly add the vinegar and the lemon juice, followed by the remainder of the olive oil. Transfer the sauce to a small bowl and refrigerate it until ready to use. The sauce will keep for at least 10 days when properly stored.

polenta with italian sausages

This simple dish is redolent with classic Italian flavors. For years, I have referred to it as "Mean Streets Sausage and Polenta," because I've served it numerous times after—and a couple of times during— the classic 1970s movie.

IN A HEAVY frying pan, brown the sausages in the olive oil, remove them from the pan, and set aside. Add the onion and sauté over medium heat until fragrant and translucent, about 15 minutes. Add the minced garlic and cook for an additional 2 minutes. Add the tomatoes, breaking up the tomatoes with a fork as you stir. Stir in the tomato sauce, wine, oregano, thyme, red pepper flakes, and salt and pepper to taste, and simmer over low heat for 20 minutes. Cut the sausages into $1/2$-inch rounds, add them to the sauce, and simmer for another 20 minutes. Taste and correct the seasoning.

While the sauce is cooking prepare the polenta. Before pouring it into a mold, brush the mold with extra virgin olive oil, then press 2 garlic cloves into the mold, and use a brush to spread the garlic evenly over the surface. Sprinkle the cayenne pepper over the surface of the mold, and then pour in the hot polenta. Let it set up in a warm place for 15 minutes before serving.

To serve, invert the hot polenta onto a large serving platter and surround with the sausages in their sauce. Dust with the grated cheese and serve immediately.

1 sweet red pepper, roasted, peeled, and seeded

1 small tomato, peeled, seeded, and chopped

$1\frac{1}{4}$ cup extra virgin olive oil

5 garlic cloves

$1/4$ cup red wine vinegar

Juice of 1 lemon

Serves 4–6

1 pound hot Italian sausage

2–3 tablespoons olive oil

1 medium yellow onion, diced

6 garlic cloves, minced

2 cups canned whole tomatoes, with juice

1 cup tomato sauce

$1/2$ cup red wine

1 teaspoon minced oregano (or $1/2$ teaspoon dried)

1 teaspoon minced thyme leaves (or $1/4$ teaspoon dried)

$1/4$ teaspoon crushed red pepper flakes

Kosher salt and black pepper in a mill

Soft Polenta (page 22)

Extra virgin olive oil

2 garlic cloves

Scant $1/4$ teaspoon ground cayenne pepper

1 ounce Parmigiano-Reggiano, grated

polenta with sausages, apples, and mustard greens

If they are available, consider decorating the table with a bouquet of field mustard and apple blossoms. If vegetarians will be guests at your table, serve the sausages separately from the polenta, not on top, and sauté the apples in a separate skillet. The resulting sauce won't be quite as flavorful, but everyone will be well fed.

4–5 cups water

2 teaspoons kosher salt

1 cup polenta

5 teaspoons yellow mustard powder, mixed with 2 tablespoons water

4 tablespoons butter

3½ ounces Dry Jack or other hard cheese, grated

2 pounds chicken-apple sausages or other sausages of choice

Dry white wine or water

2 tart-sweet apples, peeled, cored, and cut into ¼-inch rounds

1 quart young mustard greens

PLACE 4 CUPS water in a large, heavy pot, add the salt, and whisk in the polenta. Place over a medium flame and slowly bring to a boil, stirring regularly. When the mixture begins to boil, lower the heat. Simmer the polenta, stirring constantly, until the mixture begins to thicken, about 5 minutes. Once it has thickened, stir every couple of minutes for another 5 to 6 minutes. Add half the mustard and water mixture and 2 tablespoons butter, and stir well. Taste the polenta and if it is still grainy and hard, simmer for another 5 minutes, stirring constantly. The polenta should be fairly thick but thin enough to fall from a spoon. If it is too thick, add the remaining water, ¼ cup at a time. When the polenta is done, add the cheese and stir until it has melted. The mixture should pour easily at this point. Place in a large, shallow serving dish and set aside while preparing the sausages.

You can begin to prepare the sausages while you are cooking the polenta if you like. Place the sausages in a heavy skillet and cover with dry white wine or water. Simmer, turning the sausages once, until the liquid has evaporated. Brown the sausages evenly on all sides. Arrange them over the polenta and keep warm in a 200°F oven.

Melt the remaining butter in the skillet and sauté the apples until they are just barely tender. Arrange over the polenta and sausages. Have the mustard greens nearby in a large bowl. Stir the remaining mustard powder into the pan drippings, add a small amount of water or white wine, and deglaze the pan. Add the greens and toss until they are just wilted. Place the greens on top of the polenta, sausages, and apples, and serve immediately.

chicken livers, chorizo, and garlic with sage and shallot polenta

If you love chicken livers, you will love this dish. Authentic Spanish chorizo—made with vinegar and plenty of garlic—provide enticing flavor and aroma. If chorizos aren't available, use linguiça, kielbasa, or ask your butcher for the best substitute.

Serves 4–6

PREPARE THE POLENTA and while it is cooking, prepare the livers and chorizo. In a medium sauté pan, heat the olive oil and sauté the onion over low heat until it is soft and fragrant, about 15 minutes. Add the chorizo and sauté for about 15 minutes until most of its fat is rendered. Drain away excess fat, leaving about 2 tablespoons in the pan, and return the pan to the heat. Add the garlic, and sauté for 2 minutes. Increase the heat to medium, add the livers to the pan and sauté quickly until the livers just barely lose their pink color. Add the thyme, sage, allspice, and lemon juice, taste, and season with salt and pepper. Remove from the heat.

Pour the polenta onto a large serving platter, spoon the livers over the polenta, garnish with fresh herbs, and serve immediately.

Sage-Shallot Polenta (page 27)

Olive oil

1 small yellow onion, minced

1/2 pound chorizo

8 garlic cloves, minced

1 1/2 pounds chicken livers, rinsed, dried, trimmed, and sliced

1 teaspoon minced thyme leaves

1/2 teaspoon minced sage

1/2 teaspoon ground allspice

Juice of 1 lemon

Kosher salt and black pepper in a mill

Sprigs of fresh herbs, for garnish

curried polenta with chicken-apple sausages and chutney sauce

Serves 4

Several companies are making a chicken sausage seasoned with Indian curry spices. If they are not available in your area, any light chicken or duck sausage will do. Alternately, this polenta can be served without the sausages as a vegetarian dish. Just be sure to serve plenty of chutney and yogurt on the side. Slices of grilled eggplant would make an excellent accompaniment to the vegetarian version.

4 cups cold water

1 cup polenta

1–3 teaspoons hot curry powder, to taste

1 teaspoon kosher salt

$1/2$ teaspoon turmeric

1 teaspoon ground ginger or $1/2$-inch piece fresh ginger, peeled and grated

1 teaspoon ground cumin

$1/4$ teaspoon cayenne pepper, plus more for the pan

1 tablespoon butter

$1^1/4$ cups plain yogurt

Olive oil

Sausages
1 pound (approximately 8) East Indian chicken-apple sausages

2 cups white wine

2 tablespoons olive oil

$1/2$–1 cup chutney, such as Major Grey's

TO MAKE THE polenta, fill a heavy pot with the cold water and stir in the polenta. Turn the burner to medium, add the curry powder and salt, and stir the polenta until it comes to a boil. Reduce the heat and continue to stir, adding the remaining spices and butter, until the polenta is thick and bubbly, 30 to 40 minutes, adding additional water as necessary. Taste and remove from the heat when the texture is tender and creamy. Stir in $3/4$ cup yogurt.

Coat a 10-inch tart pan that has a removable bottom with olive oil and sprinkle it lightly with cayenne pepper. Pour in the polenta, smooth it out evenly, and keep it warm while it sets up.

Meanwhile, place the sausages in a heavy frying pan with 1 cup wine. Simmer for about 8 minutes, or until the wine has evaporated. Add the olive oil to the pan and brown the sausages. Remove them from the pan and keep them hot. Add the remaining cup of wine, turn the heat to high, loosen the pan drippings, and reduce the wine by about half. Stir in 1/2 cup chutney and heat thoroughly. Remove the polenta from the tart pan and place on a serving platter. Cut into 8 wedges. Top each wedge with a sausage and pour sauce over all. Serve immediately with the remaining chutney and yogurt on the side.

side dishes and accompaniments

polenta fries

Polenta fries: You find them on pricey restaurant menus, in articles about polenta, in recipes on the backs of cornmeal packages. There is no real mystery to polenta fries; they are simply cooked cornmeal, lightly seasoned and allowed to set up until firm. They are then sliced into strips, deep fried, and served with a savory condiment such as gorgonzola or chèvre mixed with cream, marinara sauce, or if you must, ketchup. I like them dusted with finely grated Parmigiano-Reggiano and sprinkled with a bit of cayenne pepper and coarse-grained salt.

Makes approximately 7 1/2 dozen

Firm Polenta (page 29; see Note)

Olive oil

CUT FIRM polenta into strips 3/4-inch wide and 3 inches long (use a ruler or other straight-edge to guide you).

Pour 2 to 3 inches of oil into a heavy, wide, deep pot. Set over medium-high heat and heat to 350°F. Carefully add polenta strips to the hot oil, taking care not to overcrowd the pot. Use a long-handled fork to separate the strips so they do not stick. Cook, turning once or twice with a slotted spoon, until the strips are just golden brown, about 5 minutes. Use a slotted spoon to remove the fries and set them on several layers of absorbent paper (brown paper bags are ideal). Repeat until all polenta strips have been cooked. Transfer the polenta fries to a serving platter or individual serving plates, season with a bit of salt, and serve immediately.

N o t e : When preparing the firm polenta, reduce the amount of cornmeal to 2 cups, salt to 3 tablespoons, water to 8 cups, butter to 3 ounces, and cheese to 2 ounces. Use the same size (17 1/4 × 12 1/4 inches) baking sheet.

polenta spoonbread

Where does one draw the line between polenta and cornmeal, between polenta and cornbread? The boundary blurs, and I decided to draw it here with a typically American dish, spoonbread, made with a coarse-textured polenta. Serve it with any roasted or grilled meat or poultry, or as part of a hearty winter breakfast.

Serves 4 – 8

BRUSH A HEAVY cast-iron skillet with olive oil and place it in a 400°F oven. In a medium saucepan, stir together the polenta, water, buttermilk, salt, and cayenne pepper, bring the mixture to a boil, reduce the heat, and cook for 5 minutes, stirring constantly. Remove from the heat and cool slightly.

Stir together the melted butter and egg yolks; add a tablespoon or two of the polenta mixture to the egg mixture, stir, and then pour the egg mixture into the polenta, stirring well. Stir the baking powder into the batter and then quickly fold in the egg whites. Carefully remove the skillet from the oven, reduce the heat to 375°F, pour the batter into the skillet, and immediately (and carefully) return it to the oven. Bake for about 40 minutes until golden brown. Remove from the oven and serve immediately.

Olive oil

1 cup coarse-ground blue, yellow, or white polenta

2 cups water

1 cup buttermilk

1 teaspoon kosher salt

1/4 teaspoon cayenne pepper

2 tablespoons butter, melted

3 egg yolks, beaten

2 teaspoons baking powder

3 egg whites, beaten to stiff peaks

turkish polenta spoonbread

Serves 4-8

My friend Engin Akin, a journalist who lives in Istanbul, provided me with several recipes for traditional Black Sea polenta. There, two types of ground corn, gün darisi and firin darisi, are used to make several versions of a coarse, dense bread cooked on top of the stove or in the oven. Sometimes leeks, onions, spring greens, herbs, tomatoes, and small fish, fresh or pickled, are folded into the polenta batter before it is cooked. One variation, known as anchovy birds, consists of an anchovy wrapped around a small ball of polenta dough, which is then dipped in flour and fried. Here, I've combined American spoonbread techniques with flavors evocative of those in Engin's recipes to create a dense, savory polenta bread that I hope captures the spirit, if not the letter, of the Black Sea polentas. Served with yogurt, chopped tomatoes, diced cucumber, and sardines alongside, it is absolutely delicious.

1 yellow onion, minced

2 tablespoons olive oil, plus more for the pan

3/4 cup toasted corn-meal (see Resources)

1/4 cup coarse-ground polenta

1 1/2 cups water

1 cup plain lowfat (not nonfat) yogurt

1 teaspoon kosher salt

2 tablespoons butter, melted

2 egg yolks, beaten

2 tablespoons minced Italian parsley

2 tablespoons minced mint

2 tablespoons minced cilantro

2 teaspoons baking powder

2 egg whites, beaten to soft peaks

IN A SMALL skillet, sauté the onions in the olive oil, until soft and translucent, about 15 minutes, and set aside. Brush a heavy, cast-iron skillet with olive oil and place it in a 400°F oven. In a medium saucepan, stir together the cornmeal, polenta, water, yogurt, and salt, bring the mixture to a boil, reduce the heat, and cook for 5 minutes, stirring constantly. Remove from the heat and cool slightly.

Combine the sautéed onions, melted butter, and egg yolks; add a tablespoon or two of the polenta mixture to the egg mixture, stir, and then pour the egg mixture into the polenta, add the herbs, and stir well. Stir the baking powder into the batter and then quickly fold in the egg whites. Carefully remove the skillet from the oven, reduce the heat to 375°F, pour the batter into the skillet, and immediately (and carefully) return it to the oven. Bake for about 50 minutes until golden brown. Remove from the oven, turn out onto a rack, and let rest for 5 minutes before serving.

baked summer tomatoes filled with polenta

Baked tomatoes are one of my favorite side dishes, particularly as summer fades into fall and there are still plenty of plump tomatoes on the vine.

CUT OFF THE stem end of each tomato about ¼ inch down, just before you get to the wide shoulder of the tomato. Discard the stem end and with a sharp knife cut out most of the interior, being careful not to cut through the side of the tomato. Use a spoon to complete the process and make a smooth interior. Set the tomatoes, cut side down, on absorbent toweling.

Sprinkle a little salt and one or two turns of black pepper into each tomato shell and then fill each to the top with polenta. Set in a baking dish and place in a preheated 325°F oven and bake for 20 minutes until the tomatoes are tender and cooked through. Remove from the oven, garnish with sprigs of fresh herbs, and serve immediately as an accompaniment to seafood, poultry, or meat, or as part of a vegetarian meal.

Serves 8

8 medium tomatoes

½ recipe Soft Polenta (page 22), Fresh Herb Polenta (page 26), or Olive-Herb Polenta (page 27)

Kosher salt and black pepper in a mill

Sprigs of fresh herbs, for garnish

garlic broccoli with fried polenta

The combination of broccoli and polenta is common throughout Italy wherever polenta is eaten. For best results, be sure not to overcook the broccoli.

COOK THE BROCCOLI in a vegetable steamer over hot water until it is almost done, remove it from the heat, and set aside to cool briefly. Cut the polenta into 1½ × 2½-inch rectangles and fry them in a large skillet according to the instructions on page 30. Arrange the fried polenta around the outside edge of a large serving platter. Add a little olive oil to the skillet, sauté the garlic over medium heat until it is soft and fragrant, 3 to 4 minutes. Do not let it burn. Add the broccoli, toss with the garlic, and sauté until it is heated through. Season with salt and pepper, and place the broccoli in the center of the serving platter with the polenta. Serve immediately.

Serves 4–6

4–5 cups broccoli florets (save the stems for vegetable stock)

Soft Polenta (page 22), set up firm in a baking sheet

Olive oil

6 garlic cloves, very thinly sliced

Kosher salt and black pepper in a mill

baked cherry tomatoes with fried polenta triangles

Serves 4 – 6

I have been making this simple dish for more than two decades and love it just as much now as when I first gathered luscious cherry tomatoes from my garden and popped them into the oven with some garlic. When you fry the polenta triangles, dredge them in egg and flour first to make them as crispy as possible on the outside. They make an excellent accompaniment to the tomatoes.

1 quart cherry tomatoes, the sweetest available

Handful of garlic cloves

2 tablespoons snipped chives

¼ cup extra virgin olive oil

Juice of 1 lemon

Black pepper in a mill

Kosher salt

Lemon Zest Polenta (page 26), prepared for shapes (page 28)

2 tablespoons minced Italian parsley

PLACE THE TOMATOES in a baking dish, add the garlic, chives, and olive oil, and stir briefly. Add the lemon juice and several turns of black pepper, and place in a 350°F oven for 20 to 30 minutes until the tomatoes have burst open and the garlic is tender. Remove from the oven and let cool slightly. Taste and season with salt.

Cut the polenta into 3-inch triangles and fry according to the instructions on page 30. To serve, set 2 triangles on individual serving plates, spoon some of the tomatoes and their liquid over the triangles, and scatter a little Italian parsley over each portion. Serve immediately.

fried green tomatoes with cream, bacon, cilantro, and polenta

This is just the thing to enjoy in the fall, when the bounty of tomatoes that did not ripen must be used or lost to a frost.

PREHEAT THE OVEN to 300°F. Cut and discard the stem and blossom ends of the tomatoes and cut each tomato into ½-inch slices. Set the sliced tomatoes on absorbent paper. Cut the polenta into rounds just slightly larger than the tomatoes and fry them, dredging them first in egg and flour, according to the instructions on page 30. When done, set the polenta rounds on a baking sheet that has been lightly coated with olive oil.

Fry the bacon in a heavy skillet until it is golden brown and then transfer it to absorbent paper. Drain off all but 4 tablespoons bacon fat. Slice the chèvre into thin rounds and set it aside. Crumble the bacon.

Season the polenta with salt and pepper, and dredge each slice of tomato in the mixture. Fry the tomatoes in the remaining bacon fat over medium heat until the polenta browns, about 1½ minutes on each side. Set a slice of tomato on top of a polenta round and top it with a slice of the chèvre. Bake until the cheese is melted, 5 to 7 minutes.

Working quickly, pour the cream into the frying pan, place it over medium heat, and swirl the pan until the cream is hot but not boiling. Taste, season with salt and pepper, and strain into a small bowl. Remove the tomatoes from the oven, transfer them to individual serving plates, and spoon some of the sauce over each portion. Sprinkle each portion with cilantro and bacon and serve immediately.

6 medium green tomatoes

Firm Polenta (page 29) or Chile-Cilantro Polenta (page 27), prepared for shapes (page 28)

1 egg, beaten

All-purpose flour, for dredging

Olive oil

4 slices bacon

5-ounce log chèvre

¾ cup fine-ground polenta

Kosher salt and black pepper in a mill

¾ cup heavy cream

¼ cup minced fresh cilantro

zucchini with black pepper, brown butter, and hazelnut polenta

Serves 4 – 6

In classical French cooking, brown butter is called beurre noisette, *in reference to the aroma of hazelnuts the butter gives off as it browns. Serve this fragrant combination of corn, hazelnuts, and zucchini as a light vegetarian main course or as an accompaniment to a larger meal. It is particularly good with roasted chicken. Consider, too, a salad dressed with hazelnut oil and a delicate Champagne vinegar.*

Soft Polenta (page 22)

¹/₂ cup shelled hazelnuts, lightly toasted and coarsely chopped

1 teaspoon freshly ground black pepper, plus 2 additional tablespoons

4 ounces (1 stick) butter, clarified

6 small zucchini, about 4 inches long, stem ends trimmed

Kosher salt

WHEN THE POLENTA is ready, fold in the hazelnuts and 1 teaspoon black pepper, and pour it into a 10-inch tart pan or other low, flat container rinsed in cool water, and allow the polenta to set up. Unmold the polenta onto a serving plate and keep it warm. (If you make the polenta in advance, keep it in the refrigerator and heat it in a 325°F oven for 20 minutes before cooking the zucchini.)

In a heavy, medium skillet, heat the clarified butter until it begins to take on color and give off a nutty aroma. Remove it from the heat and let it cool slightly. Cut the zucchini into ¹/₄-inch rounds. Return the pan to medium heat, add the zucchini, agitate the pan, and cook for 4 minutes only. Add the remaining black pepper, toss to coat the zucchini, remove from the heat, and season with salt to taste.

Spoon the zucchini on top of the polenta and pour any pan drippings over. Serve immediately.

polenta loaf
with pesto

A variation of this recipe appeared in my first book, A Cook's Tour of
Sonoma. *I continue to receive requests for the recipe from people who have
eaten it at a friend's and have not been able to locate the book. Even though
I sometimes shudder at the combination of dried tomatoes and pesto, an
ubiquitous pairing that has been overdone to the point of being a California
cuisine cliché, this remains one of my favorite dishes.*

Serves 4 – 6

COAT A 5-CUP decorative mold, bread pan, or quiche pan with olive oil
and set it aside. Prepare the polenta, adding the dried tomato bits as you add
the polenta to the boiling water. When the polenta is nearly ready, stir in the
garlic and both cheeses. Remove from the heat.

Pour one third of the polenta into the mold and let it sit for a minute or
two, but no more. Spread half of the pesto over the surface of the polenta, add
another third of the polenta, and repeat the process of letting the polenta rest,
then topping it with pesto. Finish with the final third of the polenta. Let the
loaf sit for at least 20 minutes, unmold it onto a serving platter, and garnish it
with basil leaves. Serve immediately.

This polenta can be made up to 2 days in advance and reheated in the
oven.

Note: If dried tomato bits are not available (see Resources, page 133), use
dried tomatoes marinated in oil. Mince or puree them and add them with the
garlic and cheese.

Extra virgin olive oil

Soft Polenta (page 22)

**$1/4$ cup dried tomato
bits (see Note)**

5 garlic cloves, pressed

**4 ounces Fontina,
Gruyère, Dry Jack, St.
George, or Parmigiano-
Reggiano, grated**

**4 ounces Gorgonzola,
crumbled**

$3/4$ cup Pesto (page 35)

Basil leaves

desserts

polenta biscotti

Corn provides both flavor and texture to these little cookies, especially if you use the wonderful unrefined corn oil from Spectrum Naturals. Look for it in natural food stores and gourmet markets.

Makes about 3½ dozen cookies

Butter

1⅓ cups all-purpose flour, plus more for the pan

1 cup medium-ground yellow polenta

¾ cup granulated sugar

1½ teaspoons baking powder

¼ teaspoon salt

3 eggs, beaten

1 tablespoon unrefined corn oil or olive oil

1 teaspoon vanilla extract

1 cup fresh corn kernels

1 egg white mixed with 1 tablespoon water

PREHEAT THE OVEN to 400°F, and lightly butter and flour a baking sheet. In the bowl of a food processor, combine the flour, polenta, sugar, baking powder, and salt, and pulse until well blended. Add the eggs, corn oil, vanilla extract, and corn kernels, and pulse until the mixture comes together as a coarse, sticky dough. Transfer the dough to a floured work surface and, using your fingers, gather it up into a ball. Cut it into 4 equal portions.

Roll each portion of dough into a rope about 10 inches long and about 2¼ to 2½ inches in diameter, incorporating any flour that the dough wants to absorb to keep it from sticking to the surface. Place the finished lengths on the baking sheet at least 4 inches apart. Just barely flatten the surface of each length, and brush the top with the egg-white mixture. Bake until the loaves just begin to color, about 20 minutes.

Remove from the oven, reduce the oven temperature to 325°F, and cool for 5 minutes. Cut into 1-inch diagonal slices, arrange on an ungreased baking sheet, and return to the oven until dry, 5 to 8 minutes. Transfer the biscotti to a wire rack to cool completely before storing in airtight containers.

almond polenta tea cake

*This light, crumbly cake is excellent with afternoon
tea or with a sweet wine for dessert.*

PREHEAT THE OVEN to 400°F.

Blanch the almonds in a pot of boiling water for 1 minute, pat dry, and peel
off the skins. Chop finely. Using a food processor, combine the almonds,
polenta, flour, sugar, salt, and 4 ounces butter. Use the remaining butter to
grease a 9-inch tart pan with a removable base. Spread the dough in the pan
and bake for 30 minutes or until light golden. Let cool slightly, remove the
bottom, and transfer the cake to a serving plate. Let it cool completely, then
sift powdered sugar over the top and serve.

Serves 6–8

1 cup almonds

1 cup polenta

¼ cup all-purpose flour

½ cup granulated
sugar

Pinch salt

4½ ounces (10 table-
spoons) unsalted but-
ter, softened

1 tablespoon powdered
sugar

polenta pudding with coconut and fresh corn

*If you like Thai sticky rice and mango, one of my favorite desserts, you will
adore this rich corn pudding. The combination of coconut milk and corn is
sensational, and the spices add an evocative yet subtle element that is simply
irresistible. Serve plain, with fresh berries, or with sliced mangoes.*

FILL THE BOTTOM part of a double boiler half full with water, bring it to
a boil, and reduce to a simmer. Meanwhile, combine the coconut cream,
coconut milk, water, sugar, and spices in a medium saucepan, and bring to a
boil. Reduce the heat to a simmer and slowly pour in the polenta, stirring all
the while. Fold in the corn, transfer the mixture to the top part of the double
boiler, cover, and set it over the bottom part. Cook until most of the liquid has
been absorbed and the polenta is tender, 1 to 1½ hours. When the polenta is
nearly done, use tongs to remove and discard the vanilla bean and cinnamon
stick. Remove from the heat, let cool to room temperature, and spoon into
individual serving dishes.

Serves 6

1 cup coconut cream

1 cup coconut milk

2 cups water

½ cup granulated
sugar

2-inch piece vanilla
bean

2-inch piece cinnamon
stick

6–8 cardamom seeds,
crushed

½ teaspoon crushed
white peppercorns

1 cup white or yellow
polenta

2 cups fresh sweet
corn kernels

127

christmas soufflé with cranberry kissel

Serves 4 – 6

1 cup granulated sugar

2 cups water

1 tablespoon minced lemon zest

1 tablespoon minced orange zest

3 cups fresh cranberries

2 teaspoons butter, softened

1 cup half-and-half

1 tablespoon minced candied lemon peel

1 tablespoon minced candied orange peel

1 tablespoon minced dried cranberries

²/₃ cup fine-ground yellow polenta

¹/₂ teaspoon kosher salt

3 eggs, separated

Kissel is a Russian custardlike berry dessert, one of the oldest ritual foods of the region, Anya von Bremzen tells us in Please to the Table. *Here, cranberry kissel has no added thickener, and its somewhat more saucelike texture makes a sweet and tangy complement to the creamy polenta soufflé spiked with candied citrus.*

PLACE ²/₃ CUP sugar, ²/₃ cup water, the lemon and orange zests, and the fresh cranberries in a heavy saucepan, and bring to a boil over medium heat, stirring occasionally. Reduce the heat and simmer until all the cranberries pop, about 5 minutes. Puree half the sauce in a blender or food processor or with an immersion blender and add the puree to the whole berries. Set aside until ready to use. The kissel can be made in advance.

To prepare the soufflé, butter a 1-quart soufflé dish with the 2 teaspoons butter and preheat the oven to 350°F. In a heavy saucepan, combine the half-and-half, remaining water, and remaining sugar, and bring it to a boil, stirring until the sugar is completely dissolved. Add the lemon peel, orange peel, and dried cranberries. Whisk in the polenta and cook, stirring constantly, until the mixture is the consistency of very thick cream, 5 to 10 minutes, depending on the age and type of polenta. Add the salt and remove from the heat.

Mix the egg yolks into the polenta one at a time and beat the egg whites until they form soft peaks. Using a rubber spatula, gently fold half the beaten egg whites into the polenta and when they are well incorporated, fold in the remaining egg whites. Pour the batter into the buttered soufflé dish, place in the oven, and bake for 30 minutes until the soufflé is lightly browned.

Remove the soufflé from the oven, drizzle a small amount of the cranberry kissel over the top, and serve the remaining kissel on the side.

polenta pound cake with four variations

This polenta, inspired by Mark Elkin, the first chef of Oliveto Restaurant in Oakland, California, is smooth and velvety. It is equally good served by itself or alongside seasonal fruit for a more elaborate dessert.

SEVERAL HOURS BEFORE making the pound cake, combine the buttermilk and lavender flowers, and refrigerate until ready to use. Strain the buttermilk and discard the lavender flowers. Stir the polenta into the buttermilk, add the rosemary, and let soak for 1 hour.

Preheat the oven to 350°F; butter and flour an 8-inch tube pan. Sift together the flour, baking powder, baking soda, and salt. Using an electric mixer, cream together the butter and sugar until light and fluffy. Add the eggs one at a time, beating well after each addition. Using a rubber spatula, add one third of the soaked polenta and one third of the dry ingredients to the butter mixture. Continue until all the ingredients have been combined. Pour the batter into the prepared pan and bake for 40 minutes until the top is just lightly golden.

Cool in the pan for 5 minutes and then turn out onto a cake rack to cool.

Variations:

- In the spring, choose the sweetest berries you can find, slice them and toss them with a little sugar, and refrigerate for at least 2 hours. Before serving, toss with 2 tablespoons balsamic vinegar and spoon over wedges of the cake.

- When summer berries—raspberries, blackberries, ollalieberries or blueberries—are at their peak, toss them with a bit of sugar and refrigerate them for at least 2 hours before serving them over wedges of the cake. For a lusciously rich dessert, top each portion with a spoonful of mascarpone.

- In the summer, peel and slice 4 or 5 ripe peaches, toss them with 4 tablespoons sugar, and a scant $1/8$ teaspoon pure vanilla extract. Refrigerate for at least 2 hours before spooning over wedges of the pound cake.

(continued)

Serves 4 – 6

$3/4$ cup buttermilk

2 tablespoons dried lavender flowers

$1/2$ cup fine- or coarse-ground polenta

1 tablespoon finely chopped rosemary

$1^5/8$ cups all-purpose flour

2 teaspoons baking powder

$3/4$ teaspoon baking soda

$1/2$ teaspoon salt

6 ounces ($1^1/2$ sticks) unsalted butter, at room temperature

$3/4$ cup granulated sugar

2 medium eggs

- In the fall or winter, peel 3 ripe pears, cut them in half, and remove their cores. Place them in a wide saucepan and add enough red wine to cover them. Poach the pears over medium-low heat until they are tender and then use a slotted spoon to transfer them to a plate or bowl. Add $^1/_2$ cup granulated sugar and 1 small sprig of fresh rosemary to the wine, increase the heat to medium, and reduce the wine until it is the consistency of syrup. Remove from the heat, discard the rosemary sprig, and arrange the pears and the cake on a large platter. Drizzle the sauce over all and serve immediately.

Pear Tart with a Polenta Crust

Delicate flavors and textures make this tart a pleasant alternative to heavier desserts; it is particularly delicious accompanied by a raspberry, lemon, or mint sorbet, with Gorgonzola alongside.

Serves 6 – 8

4 ounces (1 stick) butter, at room temperature, plus 3 tablespoons

$^1/_2$ cup sugar

1 cup fine- or medium-ground polenta

$^1/_2$ teaspoon salt

2 eggs, at room temperature

1$^1/_2$ cups all-purpose flour

2 large or 3 medium ripe pears, peeled, cored, and sliced $^1/_4$ inch thick

Fresh mint leaves, for garnish

IN A MEDIUM bowl, blend the 1 stick butter and the sugar together. Add the polenta, salt, and eggs, and beat until smooth. Stir in the flour. Knead lightly on a floured work surface for 2 minutes, cut into 2 pieces, wrap in plastic, and chill for 20 minutes. Remove from the refrigerator and roll out one piece into a 10-inch circle, and reserve the second piece to make another tart. Press the crust into a 10-inch tart pan, place in a preheated 350°F oven, and bake for 7 minutes. Remove from the oven and set aside to cool. Reduce the heat to 325°F.

Melt the remaining butter in a skillet and sauté the sliced pears until they just begin to color. Remove from the heat and arrange the pears over the surface of the tart shell, overlapping them in 2 concentric circles. Return to the oven and bake until the pears are completely tender and the edges of the crust just begin to color. Remove from the oven and let cool for 10 minutes before serving. Cut into wedges, garnish each piece with a mint leaf, and serve.

glossary

Dried Corn Products and Traditional Polenta Ingredients

Atole cornmeal that is finely ground, toasted, and added to liquid to make a beverage; Native Americans relied upon it as an essential food for the ailing; today, it is common in Mexico and throughout the American Southwest.

Buckwheat flour the primary ingredient in polenta nera; a traditional ingredient in polenta taragna, to which it adds a depth of flavor and a slightly denser texture than polenta made exclusively with corn.

Chestnut flour finely ground chestnuts, once a common ingredient for making polenta.

Chick-pea flour finely ground dried chick-peas; cooked into a porridge or pudding similar to contemporary polenta.

Cornbread an American quick bread made with coarse- or fine-ground cornmeal, milk, eggs, baking powder, and various flavorings.

Corn flour dent corn that has been dried, finely ground, and sifted to produce a very fine powder; used primarily in commercial baking and to produce wheatless pasta.

Cornmeal, blue a stone-ground cornmeal made from one of several varieties of blue corn; has considerably more protein—about 20 percent—and sometimes more flavor than yellow cornmeal.

Cornmeal, stone ground corn that is milled between stones rather than the more common steel rollers; generally contains the germ, which adds flavor but shortens shelf life.

Farinata in Tuscany, a polenta soup served plain, with vegetables, or with sausages.

Firin darisi a delicate cornmeal from Turkey; corn is oven dried before being stone ground.

Grano saraceno the name given to buckwheat by the Italians, in reference to the Saracens, who first brought the grain to Italy.

Granoturco an early name for corn, because of its entry through the port of Venice, where trade with Turkey was quite active.

Grits the largest of the resulting granules when the bran and germ are removed and the endosperm of the corn kernel is ground; common in the American South.

Gün darisi Turkish cornmeal, dried in the shade and then ground.

Hominy whole kernels of dent or flint corn; outer hulls have been removed with lime water; available dried, frozen, or canned in water.

Kalderash savory corn cakes of Rumania and Hungary.

Las pous in the Périgord in France, polenta is named for the sound it makes as it sputters, said to be similar to the mutterings of a sleeping person.

Maize the traditional generic name for America's native grain.

Masa a somewhat coarse flour made from partially cooked and ground hominy, used to make corn tortillas.

Masa harina Mexican-style corn flour, used to make tamales.

Paiolo, traditional the traditional pot for cooking polenta in Italy; made of unlined copper with a concave bottom and a long handle, which allowed the cook to hold it over a wood fire.

Paiolo, motorized a contemporary compromise; a pot is fitted with a spatula that is turned by a motorized crank that provides for hands-off, continuous stirring of polenta.

Pellagra a serious chronic ailment caused by niacin deficiency; common in poor populations that relied upon corn products—i.e., polenta—as their primary food; caused polenta to be outlawed because before the discovery of vitamins, the disease being blamed on the consumption of polenta rather than on corn's lack of niacin; symptoms include digestive problems, skin eruptions, nervous disorders, and mental deterioration.

Polenta flour in Turkey this refers to a mixture of gün darisi and firin darisi.

Polenta, instant polenta that has been cooked, dehydrated, and ground; rehydrates quickly, with considerable loss of texture and flavor.

Polente au bâton the name for traditional polenta in the Savoie in eastern France; the technique is virtually the same as the Italian; the name refers to the constant stirring with a large stick or baton.

Polentina in Italy, refers to simple polenta soup.

Popcorn one of the six most common varieties of corn, with a high starch and moisture content that expands when heated.

Posole dried or frozen hominy, widely used in southwestern cooking.

Puliszka the traditional cornmeal puddings and cakes of Transylvania.

Suppawn another name for porridge, polenta, or cornmeal mush, this one from the northeast United States where Dutch settlers were introduced to corn by the Native Americans.

resources

Polenta and Other Dried Corn Products:

ADAMS MILLING COMPANY, INC.
Route 1, Box 248
Midland City, AL 36350
800-239-4233
Stone-ground yellow and white cornmeal

CARPENTER'S GRIST MILL
Moonstone Beach Road
Perryville, RI 02879
401-783-5483
Whitecap flint cornmeal

GRAY'S GRISTMILL
P.O. Box 422
Adamsville, RI 02801
508-636-6075
Organic, stone-ground extra-coarse polenta

THE GREAT VALLEY MILLS
1774 County Line Road
Barto, PA 19504
800-688-6455
Selection of coarse and fine cornmeals, including an excellent toasted cornmeal

GUISTO'S
241 East Harris Avenue
South San Francisco, CA 94080
415-873-6566
This purveyor of organically grown whole grain flours offers an excellent polenta. Wholesale only.

MORGAN'S MILLS
168 Payson Road
Union, ME 04862
207-785-4900
Stone-ground coarse and fine cornmeals

NATURE'S PANTRY
P.O. Box 1913
Sonoma, CA 95476-1913
707-938-5174 (fax and phone)
Mail-order catalog includes Moretti polenta from Italy, heirloom dried beans, chiles, olive oil, and other specialty products, nearly all organic. Intelligent cookbook selection, too.

THE POLENTA COMPANY
139 Mitchell Avenue, #225
South San Francisco, CA 94080
Ed Fleming
Producers of Golden Pheasant Polenta. Wholesale only.

Extra Virgin Olive Oil and Other Italian Products:

CORTI BROTHERS
5810 Folsom Boulevard
Sacramento, CA 95819
916-736-3800
Excellent selection of polentas, extra virgin olive oils, authentic balsamic vinegars, and other Italian products. Will ship.

KATZ AND COMPANY
101 South Coombs, Y-3
Napa, CA 94559
800-455-2305
Mail-order source for organic polenta, artisan olive oils and vinegars from California and Europe; a well-chosen selection of books and other culinary treasures, too.

SUTTON PLACE GOURMET
800-346-8763
A chain of high-end gourmet markets (eleven in the Washington D.C. area; one in New York State); catalog and mail order.

TODARO BROS.
557 Second Avenue
New York, NY 10016
212-679-7766
An excellent array of Italian products, from ingredients to the occasional motorized polenta pot. Mail order.

ZINGERMAN'S DELICATESSEN
422 Detroit Street
Ann Arbor, MI 48104
313-663-DELI
Another excellent source for Italian products and other imports. Mail-order catalog.

Specialty Garlic:

SUNSHINE FARMS
26653 River Road
Cloverdale, CA 95425
Egmont Tripp grows more than three dozen varieties of garlic at his organic farm in northern Sonoma County. All are available by mail order, and there's a Garlic-of-the-Month Club, too.

Dried Tomato Products:

TIMBER CREST FARMS
4791 Dry Creek Road
Healdsburg, CA 95448
707-433-8251
Mail-order source for marinated dried tomatoes, dried tomato bits, and other products.

bibliography

Aaron, Chester. *Garlic Is Life: A Memoir with Recipes.* Berkeley, CA: Ten Speed Press, 1996.

Cole, Rosalind. *Of Soda Bread and Guinness.* New York: Bobbs-Merrill, 1973.

Cunningham, Marion. *The Breakfast Book.* New York: Knopf, 1987.

Della Croce, Julia. *Antipasti.* San Francisco: Chronicle Books, 1993.

Field, Carol. *Celebrating Italy.* New York: Morrow, 1990.

———. *Italy in Small Bites.* New York: Morrow, 1993.

Fisher, M.F.K. *The Art of Eating.* New York: World, 1954.

Franey, Pierre, and Richard Flaste. *Pierre Franey's Cooking in France.* New York: Knopf, 1994.

Fussell, Betty. *The Story of Corn.* New York: Knopf, 1992.

———. *Crazy for Corn.* New York: HarperCollins, 1995.

Goldstein, Darra. *The Georgian Feast.* New York: HarperCollins, 1993.

Grey, Patience. *Honey from a Weed.* San Francisco: North Point Press, 1990.

Jones, Evan. *Epicurean Delight: The Life and Times of James Beard.* New York: Simon and Schuster, 1990.

———. *The World of Cheese.* New York: Alfred A. Knopf, 1976.

Jordan, Michele Anna. *The Good Cook's Book of Oil and Vinegar.* Reading, MA: Addison-Wesley, 1992.

———. *The Good Cook's Book of Mustard.* Reading, MA: Addison-Wesley, 1992.

———. *The Good Cook's Book of Tomatoes.* Reading, MA: Addison-Wesley, 1992.

Kamman, Madeline. *Savoie: The Land, People, and Food of the French Alps.* New York: Macmillan, 1989.

Kasper, Lynne Rossetto. *The Splendid Table.* New York: Morrow, 1992.

Liri, Clotilde. *La Polenta Ricette e Tradizioni.* Verona: Demetra, 1991.

McGee, Harold. *On Food and Cooking.* New York: Charles Scribner's Sons, 1984.

Marcolini, Piero. *Polenta Gnocchi Tortellini Storia, Leggende, Curiosità.* Verona: PAF.

Marshall, Lydie. *Chez Nous: Home Cooking from the South of France.* New York: HarperCollins, 1995.

Massara, Elena Previde. *Il Grande Libro della Polenta.*

Milioni, Stefano. *Columbus Menu.* New York: Italian Trade Commission, 1992.

Root, Waverley. *The Food of Italy.* New York: Vintage, 1977.

Shapiro, Laura. *Perfection Salad.* San Francisco: North Point Press, 1995.

von Bremzen, Anya, and John Welchman. *Please to the Table.* New York: Workman, 1990.

Waters, Alice. *Chez Parisse Vegetables.* New York: HarperCollins, 1996.

Willinger, Faith. *Red, White & Greens.* New York: HarperCollins, 1996.

Wolfert, Paula. *The Cooking of South-West France.* Garden City, NY: Dial Press, 1983.

Index